Favorite Wildflowers in Cross-Stitch

48 Charted Designs

by

Claire Bryant

Dover Publications, Inc.
New York

Copyright © 1987 by Claire Bryant.
All rights reserved under Pan American and International Copyright Conventions.

Published in Canada by General Publishing Company, Ltd., 30 Lesmill Road, Don Mills, Toronto, Ontario.
Published in the United Kingdom by Constable and Company, Ltd., 10 Orange Street, London WC2H 7EG.

Favorite Wildflowers in Cross-Stitch: 48 Charted Designs is a new work, first published by Dover Publications, Inc., in 1987.

Manufactured in the United States of America
Dover Publications, Inc., 31 East 2nd Street, Mineola, N.Y. 11501

Library of Congress Cataloging-in-Publication Data

Bryant, Claire.
   Favorite wildflowers in cross-stitch.

  (Dover needlework series)
   1. Cross-stitch—Patterns. 2. Decoration and ornament—Plant forms.
3. Wild flowers in art. I. Title. II. Series.
TT778.C76B79   1987   746.44   86-24285
ISBN 0-486-25319-8

Introduction

Wildflowers are among the best loved flowers in the world and have long been a favorite with needleworkers. Wildflowers have often been used to symbolize a specific country, state or region for, not only do they add beauty and color to the landscape, but they have a strong emotional appeal as well.

This volume presents forty-eight American wildflowers, ranging from the short-lived flowers of the saguaro cactus to the fragrant blooms of the gardenia and from the delicate lilac of the sea holly to the vivid red of the Indian paintbrush.

The flowers are arranged by geographic region—the desert, the mountains, the seashore and the tropics—with twelve flowers representing each region. No matter what part of the country you live in, you are sure to find a wildflower from your area.

The designs can be used singly to make pictures, pillows, one-of-a-kind clothing and table linens, or they can be combined for even more variety. Embroider a sampler of wildflowers or crochet an afghan with a different flower on each block—the possibilities are endless.

These designs were originally created for counted cross-stitch, but they are easily translated into other needlework techniques. Keep in mind that the finished piece will not be the same size as the charted design unless you are working on fabric or canvas with the same number of threads per inch as the chart has squares per inch. With knitting and crocheting, the size will vary according to the number of stitches per inch.

COUNTED CROSS-STITCH

MATERIALS

1. **Needles.** A small blunt tapestry needle, No. 24 or No. 26.
2. **Fabric.** Evenweave linen, cotton, wool or synthetic fabrics all work well. The most popular fabrics are aida cloth, linen and hardanger cloth. Cotton aida is most commonly available in 18 threads-per-inch, 14 threads-per-inch and 11 threads-per-inch (14-count is the most popular size). Evenweave linen comes in a variety of threads-per-inch. To work cross-stitch on linen involves a slightly different technique (see page 5). Thirty thread-per-inch linen will result in a stitch about the same size as 14-count aida. Hardanger cloth has 22 threads to the inch and is available in cotton or linen. The amount of fabric needed depends on the size of the cross-stitch design. To determine yardage, divide the number of stitches in the design by the thread-count of the fabric. For example: If a design 112 squares wide by 140 squares deep is worked on a 14-count fabric, divide 112 by 14 (=8), and 140 by 14 (=10). The design will measure 8" × 10". The same design worked on 22-count fabric measures about 5" × 6½".
3. **Threads and Yarns.** Six-strand embroidery floss, crewel wool, Danish Flower Thread, pearl cotton or metallic threads all work well for cross-stitch. DMC Embroidery Floss has been used to color-code the patterns in this volume; a conversion chart for Royal Mouliné Six-Strand Embroidery Floss from Coats & Clark, and Anchor Embroidery Floss from Susan Bates appears on page 32. Crewel wool works well on evenweave wool fabric. Danish Flower Thread is a thicker thread with a matte finish, one strand equaling two of embroidery floss.
4. **Embroidery Hoop.** A wooden or plastic 4", 5" or 6" round or oval hoop with a screw-type tension adjuster works best for cross-stitch.
5. **Scissors.** A pair of sharp embroidery scissors is essential to all embroidery.

PREPARING TO WORK

To prevent raveling, either whip stitch or machine-stitch the outer edges of the fabric.

Locate the exact center of the chart. Establish the center of the fabric by folding it in half first vertically, then horizontally. The center stitch of the chart falls where the creases of the fabric meet. Mark the fabric center with a basting thread.

It is best to begin cross-stitch at the top of the design. To establish the top, count the squares up from the center of the chart, and the corresponding number of holes up from the center of the fabric.

Place the fabric tautly in the embroidery hoop, for tension makes it easier to push the needle through the holes without piercing the fibers. While working continue to retighten the fabric as necessary.

When working with multiple strands (such as embroidery floss) always separate (strand) the thread before beginning to stitch. This one small step allows for better coverage of the fabric. When you need more than one thread in the needle, use separate strands and do not double the thread. (For example: If you need four strands, use four separated strands.) Thread has a nap (just as fabrics do) and can be felt to be smoother in one direction than the other. Always work with the nap (the smooth side) pointing down.

For 14-count aida and 30-count linen, work with two strands of six-strand floss. For more texture, use more thread; for a flatter look, use less thread.

EMBROIDERY

To begin, fasten the thread with a waste knot and hold a short length of thread on the underside of the work, anchoring it with the first few stitches (*Diagram 1*). When the thread end is securely in place, clip the knot.

DIAGRAM 1
Reverse side of work

To stitch, push the needle up through a hole in the fabric, cross the thread intersection (or square) on a left-to-right diagonal (*Diagram 2*). Half the stitch is now completed.

Next, cross back, right to left, forming an X (*Diagram 3*).

DIAGRAM 2

DIAGRAM 3

DIAGRAM 4

Work all the same color stitches on one row, then cross back, completing the X's (*Diagram 4*).

Some needleworkers prefer to cross each stitch as they come to it. This method also works, but be sure all of the top stitches are slanted in the same direction. Isolated stitches must be crossed as they are worked. Vertical stitches are crossed as shown in *Diagram 5*.

DIAGRAM 5

At the top, work horizontal rows of a single color, left to right. This method allows you to go from an unoccupied space to an occupied space (working from an empty hole to a filled one), making ruffling of the floss less likely. Holes are used more than once, and all stitches "hold hands" unless a space is indicated on the chart. Hold the work upright throughout (do not turn as with many needlepoint stitches).

When carrying the thread from one area to another, run the needle under a few stitches on the wrong side. Do not carry thread across an open expanse of fabric as it will be visible from the front when the project is completed.

To end a color, weave in and out of the underside of the stitches, making a scallop stitch or two for extra security (*Diagram 6*). When possible, end in the same direction in which you were working, jumping up a row if necessary (*Diagram 7*). This prevents holes caused by stitches being pulled in two directions. Trim the thread ends closely and do not leave any tails or knots as they will show through the fabric when the work is completed.

DIAGRAM 6
Reverse side of work

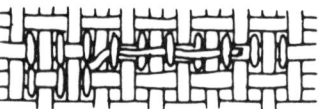

DIAGRAM 7
Reverse side of work

A number of other counted-thread stitches can be used in cross-stitch. Backstitch (*Diagram 8*) is used for outlines, face details and the like. It is worked from hole to hole, and may be stitched as a vertical, horizontal or diagonal line.

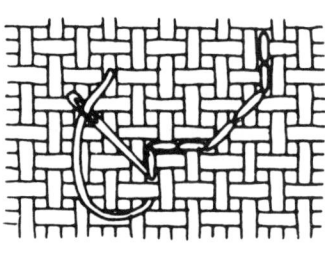

DIAGRAM 8

Straight stitch is worked over several threads (*Diagram 9*) and affords solid coverage.

DIAGRAM 9

Lazy daisy stitch, French knots and Turkey work (*Diagram 10*) are handy for special effects. All three are worked in the same manner as on regular embroidery.

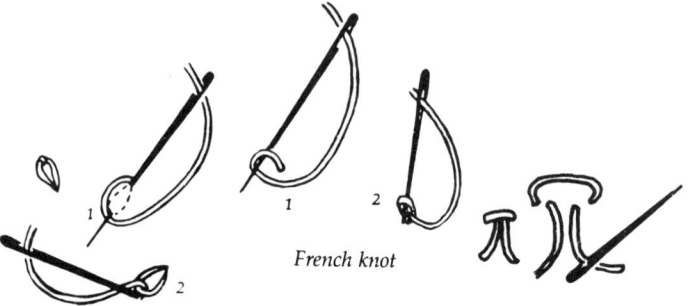

Lazy Daisy Stitch *French knot* *Turkey work*

DIAGRAM 10

Embroidery on Linen. Working on linen requires a slightly different technique. While evenweave linen is remarkably regular, there are always a few thick or thin threads. To keep the stitches even, cross-stitch is worked over two threads in each direction (*Diagram 11*).

DIAGRAM 11

As you are working over more threads, linen affords a greater variation in stitches. A half-stitch can slant in either direction and is uncrossed. A three-quarters stitch is shown in *Diagram 12*.

DIAGRAM 12

Diagram 13 shows the backstitch worked on linen.

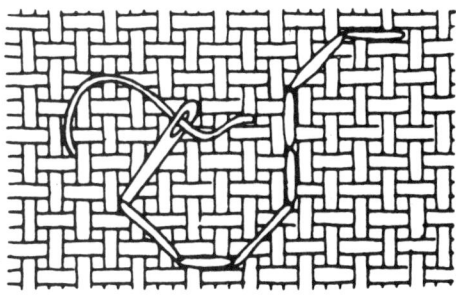

DIAGRAM 13

Embroidery on Gingham. Gingham and other checked fabrics can be used for cross-stitch. Using the fabric as a guide, work the stitches from corner to corner of each check.

Embroidery on Uneven-Weave Fabrics. If you wish to work cross-stitch on an uneven-weave fabric, baste a lightweight Penelope needlepoint canvas to the material. The design can then be stitched by working the cross-stitch over the double mesh of the canvas. When working in this manner, take care not to catch the threads of the canvas in the embroidery. After the cross-stitch is completed, remove the basting threads. With tweezers remove first the vertical threads, one strand at a time, of the needlepoint canvas, then the horizontal threads.

NEEDLEPOINT

One of the most common methods for working needlepoint is from a charted design. By simply viewing each square of a chart as a stitch on the canvas, the patterns quickly and easily translate from one technique to another.

MATERIALS

1. **Needles.** A blunt tapestry needle with a rounded tip and an elongated eye. The needle must clear the hole of the canvas without spreading the threads. For No. 10 canvas, a No. 18 needle works best.

2. **Canvas.** There are two distinct types of needlepoint canvas: single-mesh (mono canvas) and double-mesh (Penelope canvas). Single-mesh canvas, the more common of the two, is easier on the eyes as the spaces are slightly larger. Double-mesh canvas has two horizontal and two vertical threads forming each mesh. The latter is a very stable canvas on which the threads stay securely in place as the work progresses. Canvas is available in many sizes, from 5 mesh-per-inch to 18 mesh-per-inch, and even smaller. The number of mesh-per-inch will, of course, determine the dimensions of the finished needlepoint project. A 60 square × 120 square chart will measure 12" × 24" on 5 mesh-to-the-inch canvas, 5" × 10" on 12 mesh-to-the-inch canvas. The most common canvas size is 10 to the inch.

3. **Yarns.** Persian, crewel and tapestry yarns all work well on needlepoint canvas.

PREPARING TO WORK

Allow 1" to 1½" blank canvas all around. Bind the raw edges of the canvas with masking tape or machine-stitched double-fold bias tape.

There are few hard-and-fast rules on where to begin the design. It is best to complete the main motif, then fill the background as the last step.

For any guidelines you wish to draw on the canvas, take care that your marking medium is waterproof. Nonsoluble inks, acrylic paints thinned with water so as not to clog the mesh, and waterproof felt-tip pens all work well. If unsure, experiment on a scrap of canvas.

When working with multiple strands (such as Persian yarn) always separate (strand) the yarn before beginning to stitch. This one small step allows for better coverage of the canvas. When you need more than one piece of yarn in the needle, use separate strands and do not double the yarn. For example: If you need two strands of 3-ply Persian yarn, use two separated strands. Yarn has a nap (just as fabrics do) and can be felt to be smoother in one direction than the other. Always work with the nap (the smooth side) pointing down.

For 5 mesh-to-the-inch canvas, use six strands of 3-ply yarn; for 10 mesh-to-the-inch canvas, use three strands of 3-ply yarn.

STITCHING

Cut yarn lengths 18" long. Begin needlepoint by holding about 1" of loose yarn on the wrong side of the work and working the first several stitches over the loose end to secure it. To end a piece of yarn, run it under several completed stitches on the wrong side of the work.

There are hundreds of needlepoint stitch variations, but tent stitch is universally considered to be *the* needlepoint stitch. The most familiar versions of tent stitch are half-cross stitch, continental stitch and basket-weave stitch.

Half-cross stitch (*Diagram 14*) is worked from left to right. The canvas is then turned around and the return row is again stitched from left to right. Holding the needle vertically, bring it to the front of the canvas through the hole that will be the bottom of the first stitch. Keep the stitches loose for minimum distortion and good coverage. Half-cross stitch is best worked on a double-mesh canvas.

DIAGRAM 14

Continental stitch (*Diagram 15*) begins in the upper right-hand corner and is worked from right to left. The needle is slanted and always brought out a mesh ahead. The resulting stitch appears as a half-cross stitch on the front and as a slanting stitch on the back. When the row is complete, turn the canvas around to work the return row, continuing to stitch from right to left.

DIAGRAM 15

Basket-weave stitch (*Diagram 16*) begins in the upper right-hand corner with four continental stitches (two stitches worked horizontally across the top and two placed directly below the first stitch). Work diagonal rows, the first slanting up and across the canvas from right to left, and the next down and across from left to right. Moving down the canvas from left to right, the needle is in a vertical position; working in the opposite direction, the needle is horizontal. The rows interlock, creating a basket-weave pattern on the wrong side. If the stitch is not done properly, a faint ridge will show where the pattern was interrupted. On basket-weave stitch, always stop working in the middle of a row, rather than at the end, so that you will know in which direction you were working.

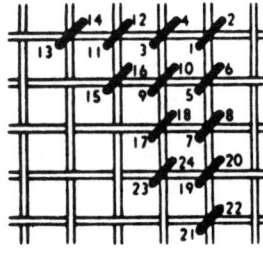
DIAGRAM 16

KNITTING

Charted designs can be worked into stockinette stitch as you are knitting, or they can be embroidered with duplicate stitch when the knitting is complete. For the former, wind the different colors of yarn on bobbins and work in the same manner as in Fair Isle knitting. A few quick Fair Isle tips: (1) Always bring up the new color yarn from under the dropped color to prevent holes. (2) Carry the color not in use loosely across the wrong side of the work, but not more than three or four stitches without twisting the yarns. If a color is not in use for more than seven or eight stitches, it is usually best to drop that color yarn and rejoin a new bobbin when the color is again needed.

CROCHET

There are a number of ways in which charts can be used for crochet. Among them are:

SINGLE CROCHET

Single crochet is often seen worked in multiple colors. When changing colors, always pick up the new color for the last yarn-over of the old color. The color not in use can be carried loosely across the back of the work for a few stitches, or you can work the single crochet over the unused color. The latter method makes for a neater appearance on the wrong side, but sometimes the old color peeks through the stitches. This method can also be applied to half-double crochet and double crochet, but keep in mind that the longer stitches will distort the design.

FILET CROCHET

This technique is nearly always worked from charts and uses only one color thread. The result is a solid-color piece with the design filled in and the background left as an open mesh. Care must be taken in selecting the design, as the longer stitch causes distortion.

AFGHAN CROCHET

The most common method here is cross-stitch worked over the afghan stitch. Complete the afghan crochet project. Then, following the chart for color placement, work cross-stitch over the squares of crochet.

OTHER CHARTED METHODS

Latch hook, Assisi embroidery, beading, cross-stitch on needlepoint canvas (a European favorite) and lace net embroidery are among the other needlework methods worked from charts.

Flowers of the Desert

◄ AZTEC

DMC #

— 367 Dark Pistachio Green backstitch
⊡ 368 Light Pistachio Green
⊘ 369 Pale Pistachio Green
◣ 726 Light Topaz
— 754 Light Peach backstitch
· White

Outline White petals with 754 Light Peach; outline Pale Pistachio Green lines in cactus and work letters with 367 Dark Pistachio Green.

CLARET CUP ►

DMC #

— 367 Dark Pistachio Green backstitch
— 320 Medium Pistachio Green backstitch
◊ 320 Medium Pistachio Green lazy daisy stitch
⊘ 368 Light Pistachio Green
V 368 Light Pistachio Green Turkey work
· 369 Pale Pistachio Green
▽ 321 Christmas Red
— 498 Dark Christmas Red backstitch
◣ 725 Topaz
— 782 Medium Topaz backstitch

Outline flowers with 498 Dark Christmas Red, flower centers with 782 Medium Topaz; outline cactus with 320 Medium Pistachio Green. Work letters with 367 Dark Pistachio Green. After other stitching has been completed, work lazy daisy stitches in centers of flowers with 320 Medium Pistachio Green; use 4 strands of 368 Light Pistachio Green to make Turkey work knots, ¼" long.

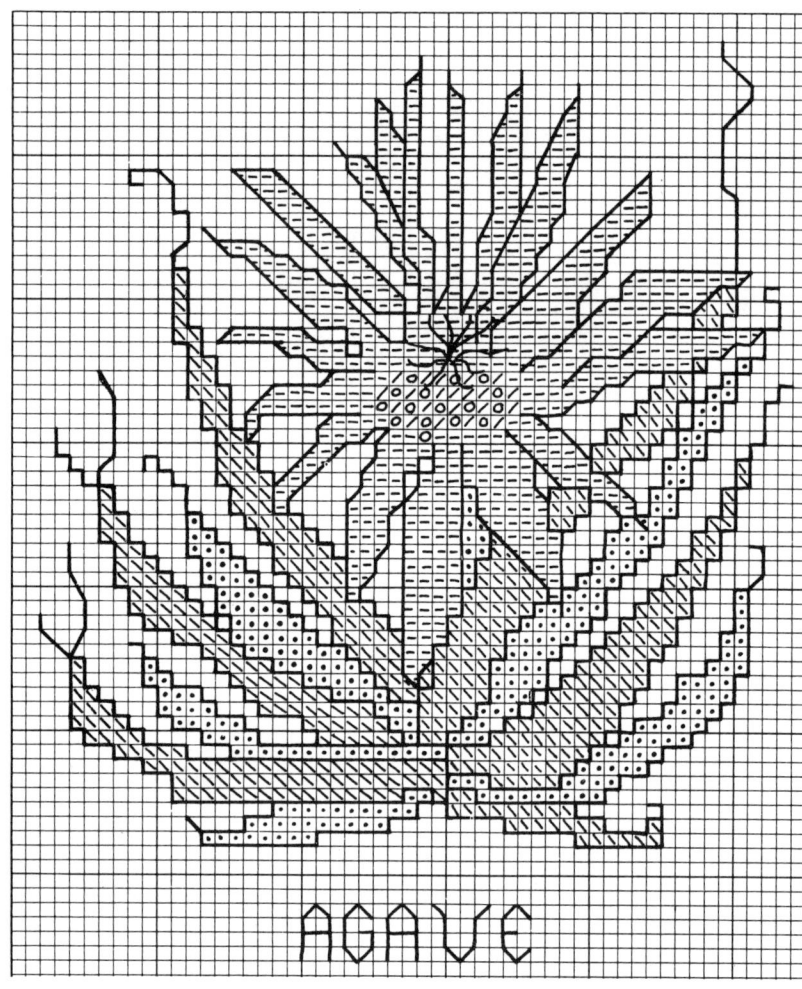

◀ AGAVE

DMC #

- ⊙ 321 Christmas Red
- — 367 Dark Pistachio Green backstitch
- — 320 Medium Pistachio Green backstitch
- ◨ 368 Light Pistachio Green
- ⊡ 369 Pale Pistachio Green
- — 780 Very Dark Topaz backstitch
- ⬚ 725 Topaz
- ⊟ 727 Very Light Topaz
- ✳ White Turkey work

Outline petals and work tips of leaves with 780 Very Dark Topaz; outline leaves with 320 Medium Pistachio Green. Work letters with 367 Dark Pistachio Green. After other stitching has been completed, use 8 strands of White to make a ½"-long Turkey work knot at center of flower.

LADYFINGER ▶

DMC #

- ✕ 209 Dark Lavender
- ◨ 211 Light Lavender
- — 367 Dark Pistachio Green backstitch
- ⋎ 367 Dark Pistachio Green Turkey work
- ⬤ 368 Light Pistachio Green
- ⊡ 369 Pale Pistachio Green
- ↑ 726 Light Topaz

Work straight stitch stamens with 726 Light Topaz; work a French knot at end of each stamen. Outline cactus and work letters with 367 Dark Pistachio Green. After other stitching has been completed, use 3 strands of 367 Dark Pistachio Green to make Turkey work knots, ¼" long.

PINK BALL ▶

DMC #

⊓	310	Black backstitch
—	367	Dark Pistachio Green backstitch
✱	367	Dark Pistachio Green Turkey work
⁄	369	Pale Pistachio Green
Ⅲ	435	Very Light Brown
—	335	Rose backstitch
V	3326	Light Rose
·	818	Baby Pink
−	727	Very Light Topaz
o		White

Work letters and lines in cactus and outline cactus with 367 Dark Pistachio Green; outline petals with 335 Rose. Work straight stitches at sides of cactus with 367 Dark Pistachio Green. After other stitching has been completed, use 6 strands of 367 Dark Pistachio Green to make Turkey work knots, ⅛" long.

◀ CROWN

DMC #

•	310	Black French knot
V	321	Christmas Red
—	498	Dark Christmas Red backstitch
—	367	Dark Pistachio Green backstitch
·	368	Light Pistachio Green
V	369	Pale Pistachio Green Turkey work
\	725	Topaz
o		White

Outline flowers with 498 Dark Christmas Red; outline cactus and work letters in backstitch with 367 Dark Pistachio Green. Work straight stitch stamens with 367 Dark Pistachio Green; work a French knot at end of each stamen with 310 Black. When other stitching has been completed, use 6 strands of 369 Pale Pistachio Green to make Turkey work knots, ½" long.

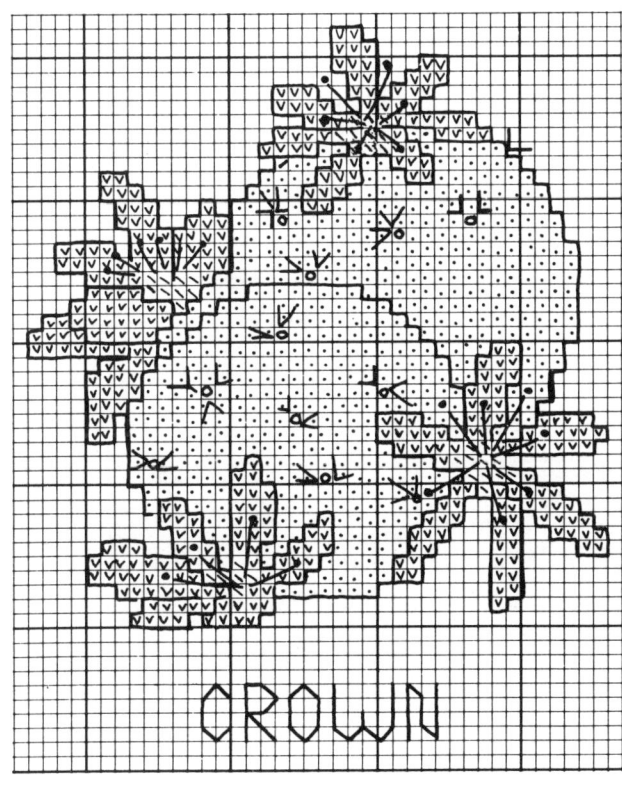

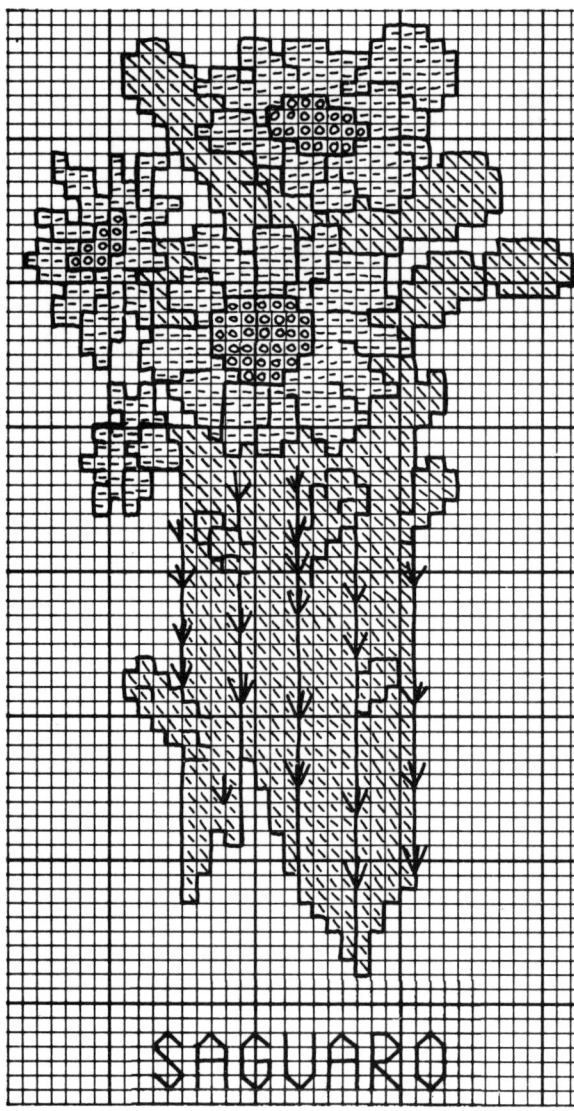

◀ SAGUARO

DMC #

- — 367 Dark Pistachio Green backstitch
- ◨ 369 Pale Pistachio Green
- V 369 Pale Pistachio Green Turkey work
- — 642 Dark Beige Gray backstitch
- ⊡ 712 Cream
- o 726 Light Topaz French knot

Outline flowers with 642 Dark Beige Gray; fill centers of flowers with 726 Light Topaz French knots. Outline cactus and work letters with 367 Dark Pistachio Green. After other stitching has been completed, use 2 strands of 369 Pale Pistachio Green to make Turkey work knots, ½" long.

JUMPING CHOLLA ▶

DMC #

- V 319 Very Dark Pistachio Green Turkey work
- — 367 Dark Pistachio Green backstitch
- — 320 Medium Pistachio Green backstitch
- ◨ 369 Pale Pistachio Green
- — 415 Pearl Gray backstitch
- • 725 Topaz French knots
- ⊡ 727 Very Light Topaz
- ⊡ White

Outline flowers with 415 Pearl Gray; outline cactus with 320 Medium Pistachio Green. Work straight stitch stamens with 319 Very Dark Pistachio Green; work a French knot at end of each stamen with 727 Topaz. Work letters with 367 Dark Pistachio Green. When other stitching has been completed, use 3 strands of 319 Very Dark Pistachio Green to make Turkey work knots, ¼" long.

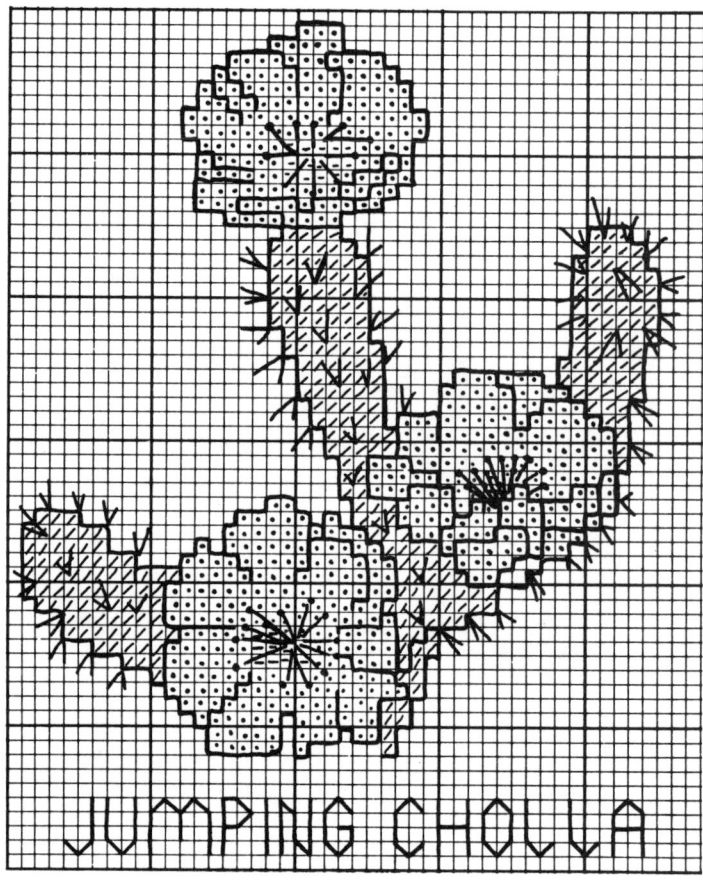

SAND DOLLAR ▶

DMC #

- ☒ 321 Christmas Red
- − 367 Dark Pistachio Green backstitch
- ╱ 369 Pale Pistachio Green
- ѵ 369 Pale Pistachio Green Turkey work
- ↘ 725 Topaz
- ✹ 726 Light Topaz lazy daisy stitch
- ⋅ 727 Very Light Topaz
- — 781 Dark Topaz backstitch
- o White French knot

Outline petals with 781 Dark Topaz; outline cactus and work letters with 367 Dark Pistachio Green. When other stitching has been completed, work lazy daisy stitches in centers of flowers with 726 Light Topaz; use 2 strands of 369 Pale Pistachio Green to make Turkey work knots, ⅛" long.

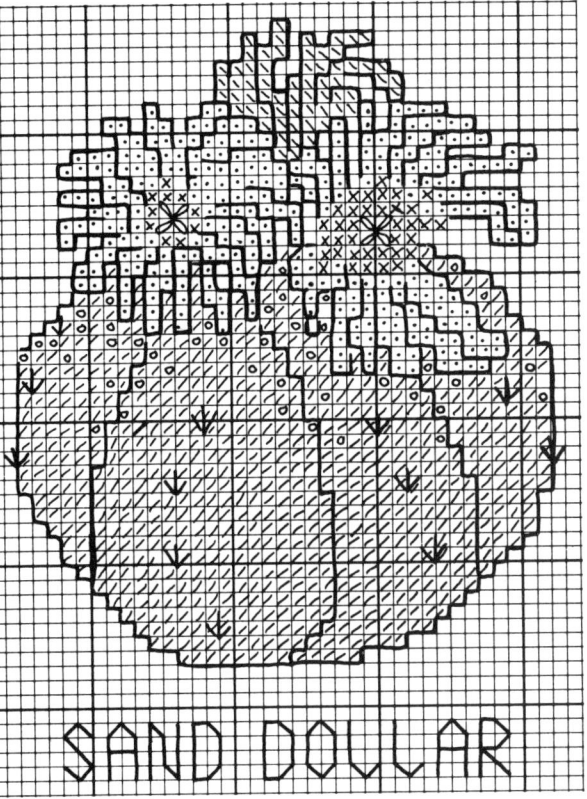

◀ GOAT'S HORN

DMC #

- ☒ 304 Medium Christmas Red
- − 367 Dark Pistachio Green backstitch
- ╱ 368 Light Pistachio Green
- ✶ 762 Very Light Pearl Gray
- o 725 Topaz French knot
- ⋅ 726 Light Topaz
- — 782 Medium Topaz backstitch
- ◊ 783 Christmas Gold lazy daisy stitch

Outline petals with 782 Medium Topaz; outline cactus and work letters with 367 Dark Pistachio Green. When other stitching has been completed, work lazy daisy stitches at center of flower with 783 Christmas Gold. With 6 strands of 762 Very Light Pearl Gray, work a ½"-long Turkey work knot at each dot, then work a French knot over each Turkey work knot.

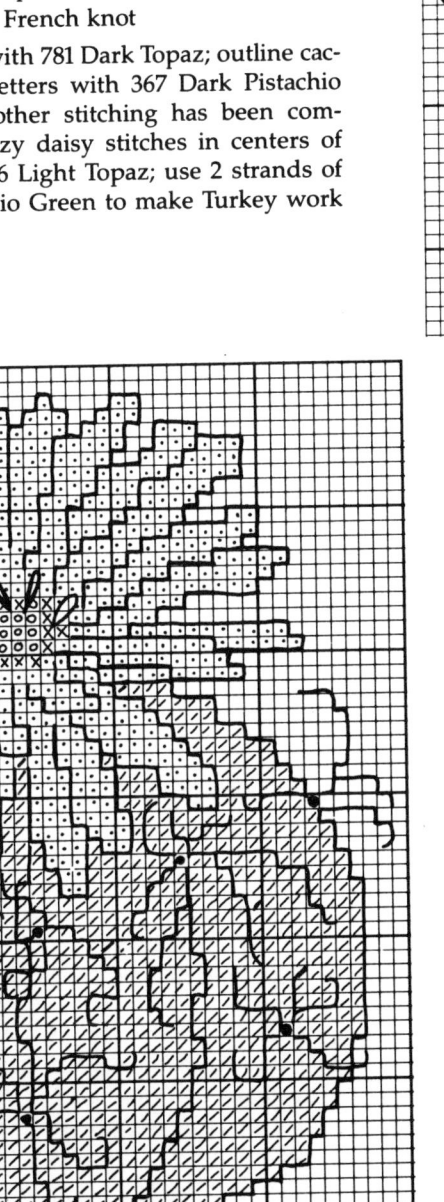

BEAVER TAIL ▶

DMC #

- ⊠ 321 Christmas Red
- − 498 Dark Christmas Red backstitch
- − 367 Dark Pistachio Green backstitch
- · 369 Pale Pistachio Green
- ◻ 369 Pale Pistachio Green French knot
- ⊠ 726 Light Topaz
- v { 320 Medium Pistachio Green } Turkey
-     { 321 Christmas Red } work

Outline petals and centers of flowers with 498 Dark Christmas Red; outline cactus and work letters with 367 Dark Pistachio Green. Work a French knot in center of each flower with 369 Pale Pistachio Green. When other stitching has been completed, use 2 strands of 320 Medium Pistachio Green and 2 strands of 321 Christmas Red combined in needle to work Turkey work knots, ¼" long.

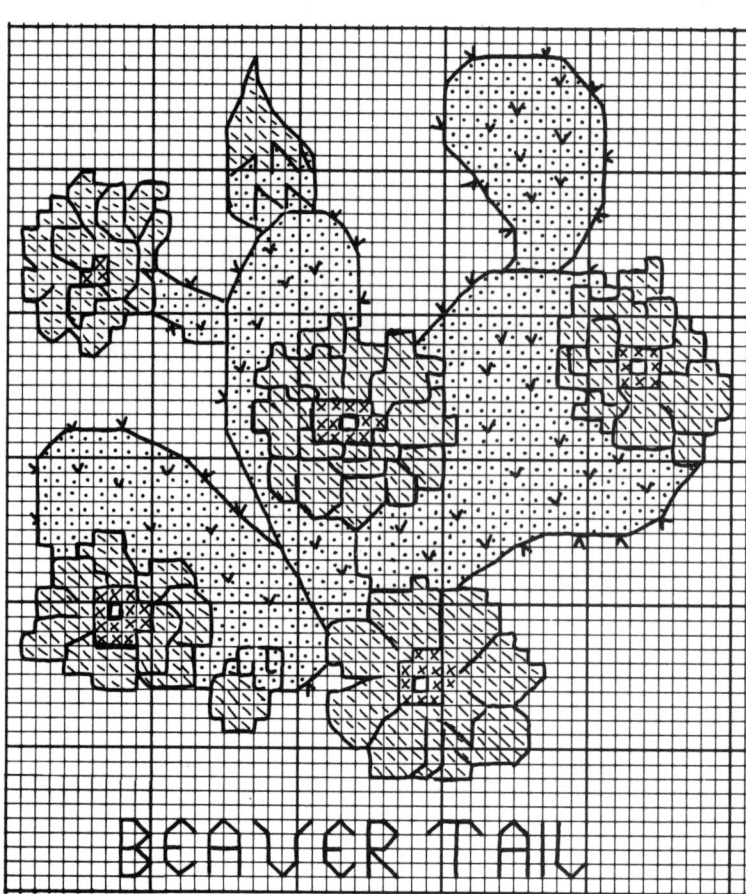

◀ RAINBOW CHIN

DMC #

- ⊠ 321 Christmas Red
- − 498 Dark Christmas Red backstitch
- − 320 Medium Pistachio Green backstitch
- − 367 Dark Pistachio Green backstitch
- ⊽ 368 Light Pistachio Green
- · 369 Pale Pistachio Green
- V 369 Pale Pistachio Green Turkey work
- o 726 Light Topaz French knots
- • White French knots

Outline petals with 498 Dark Christmas Red; outline cactus with 320 Medium Pistachio Green. Work letters with 367 Dark Pistachio Green. When other stitching has been completed, use 6 strands of 369 Pale Pistachio Green to work a ¼"-long Turkey work knot at each dot, then work a French knot with White over each Turkey work knot.

Flowers of the Mountains

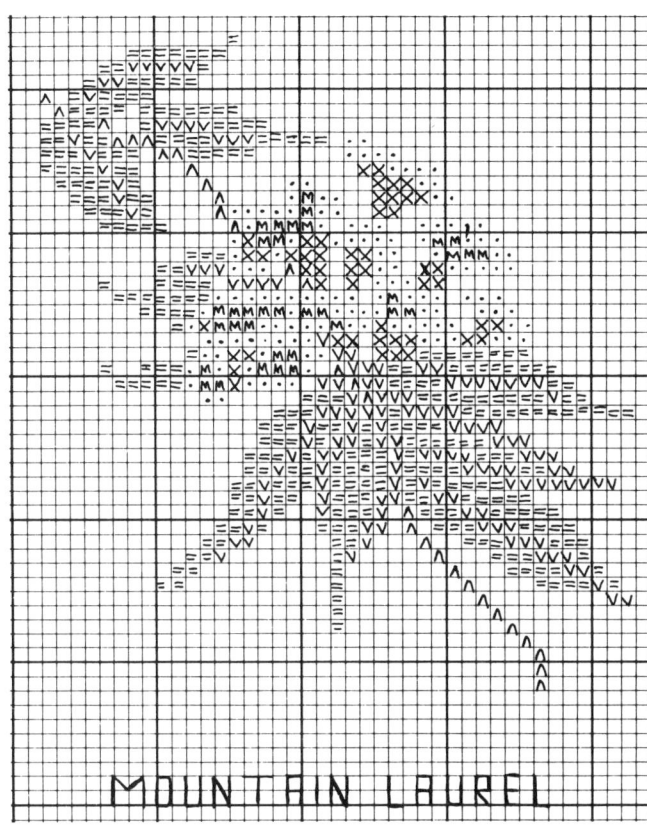

◀ **MOUNTAIN LAUREL**

DMC #

- ⌃ 300 Very Dark Mahogany
- ⋁ 367 Dark Pistachio Green
- ═ 895 Dark Christmas Green
- ⊠ 3687 Mauve
- M 3688 Medium Light Mauve
- • 3689 Light Mauve

Work letters in backstitch with 895 Dark Christmas Green.

COLUMBINE ▶

DMC #

- + 320 Medium Pistachio Green
- ⋁ 367 Dark Pistachio Green
- ═ 895 Dark Christmas Green
- o 472 Very Light Avocado Green
- ⋌ 725 Topaz
- z 793 Medium Cornflower Blue
- l 794 Light Cornflower Blue
- c White

Outline White petals in backstitch with 793 Medium Cornflower Blue; work letters in backstitch with 895 Dark Christmas Green.

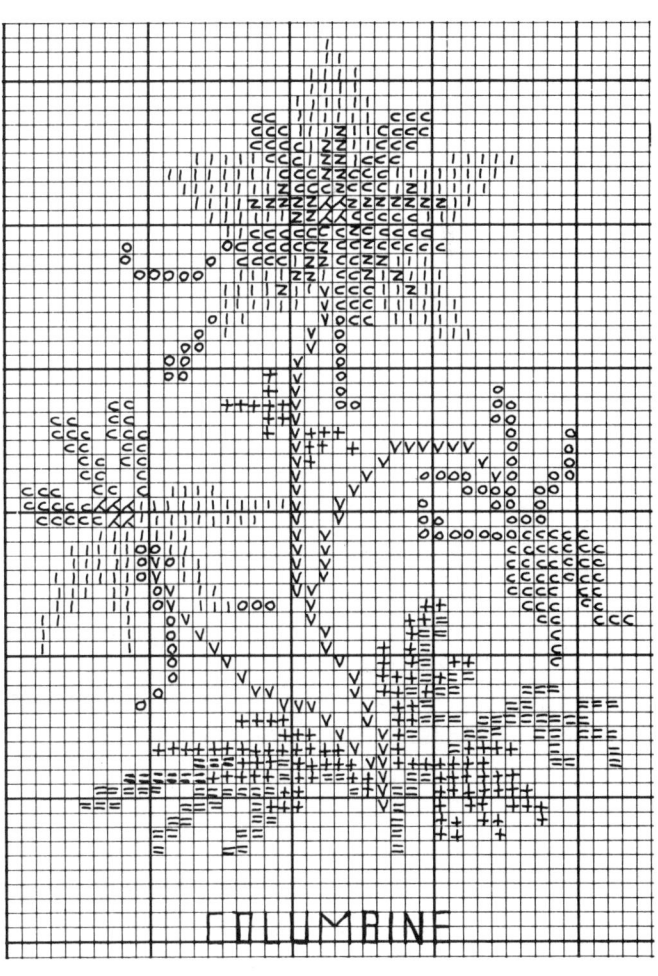

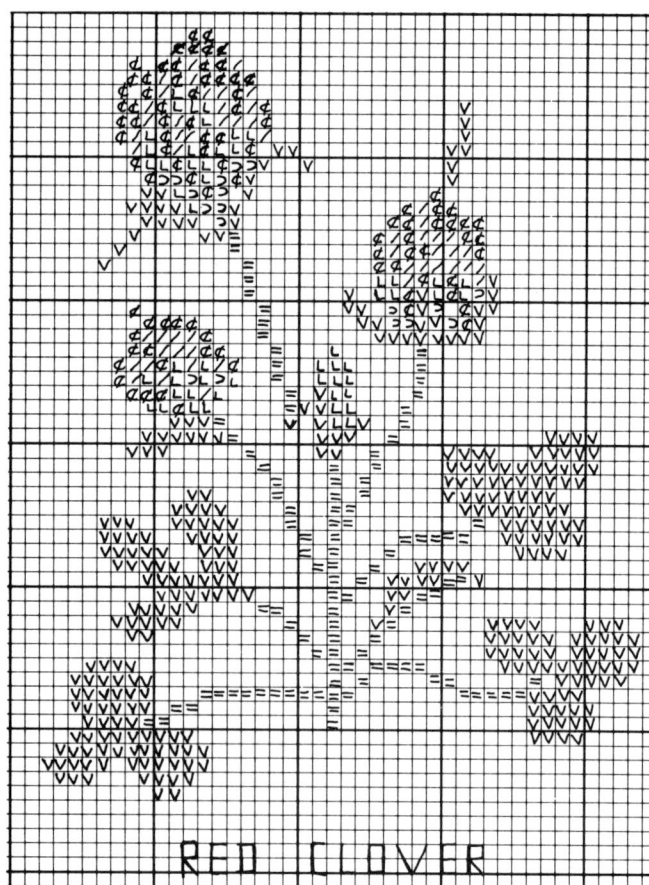

◀ RED CLOVER

DMC #

- ⊘ 350 Medium Coral
- L 351 Coral
- ⊃ 498 Dark Christmas Red
- V 367 Dark Pistachio Green
- = 895 Dark Christmas Green
- ⊘ { 351 Coral
  White
  Use 1 strand of each color

Work letters in backstitch with 895 Dark Christmas Green.

SHOOTING STAR ▶

DMC #

- ⊞ 310 Black
- + 320 Medium Pistachio Green
- V 367 Dark Pistachio Green
- = 895 Dark Christmas Green
- X 3687 Mauve
- · 3689 Light Mauve
- c White

Work letters in backstitch with 895 Dark Christmas Green.

SULFUR FLOWER ▶

DMC #

- ⊼ 300 Very Dark Mahogany
- ⊞ 320 Medium Pistachio Green
- ⊻ 367 Dark Pistachio Green
- ⊟ 471 Light Avocado Green
- ⊙ 472 Very Light Avocado Green
- ⊟ 895 Dark Christmas Green

Work letters in backstitch with 895 Dark Christmas Green.

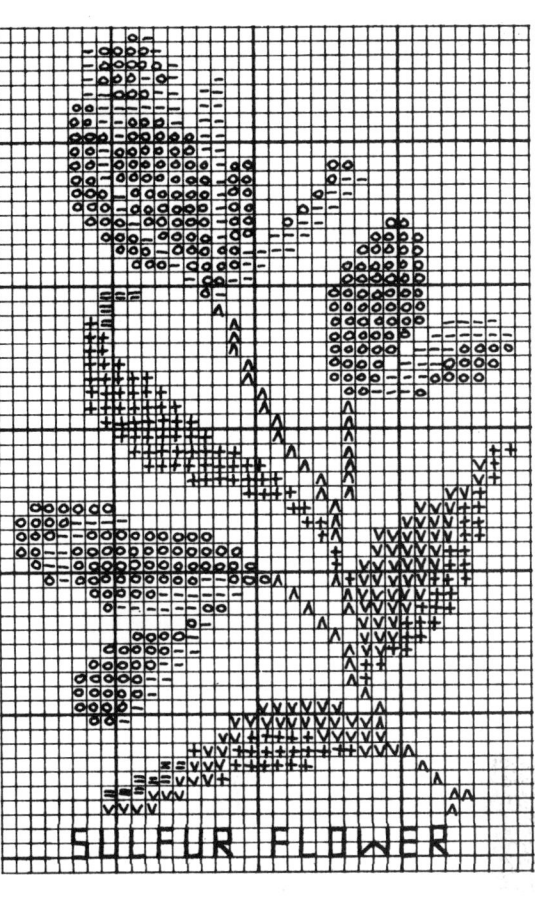

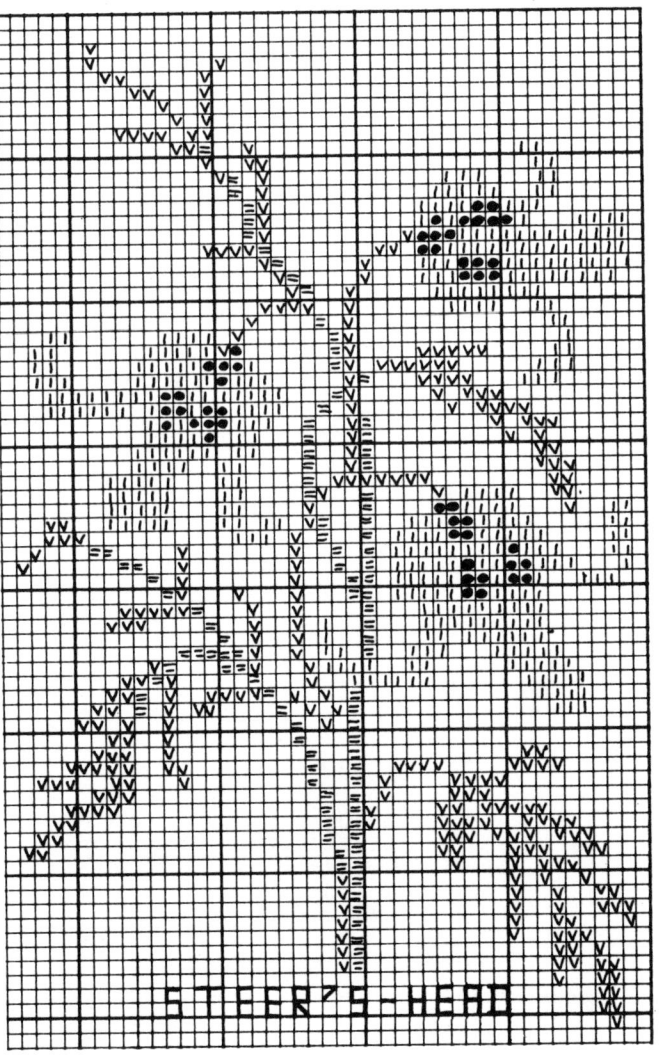

◀ STEER'S HEAD

DMC #

- ⊻ 367 Dark Pistachio Green
- ⊟ 895 Dark Christmas Green
- ⊡ 794 Light Cornflower Blue
- ⊙ { 327 Dark Antique Violet
  { 792 Dark Cornflower Blue
  Use 1 strand of each color

Work letters in backstitch with 895 Dark Christmas Green.

◀ GREEN GENTIAN

DMC #

- ⋀ 300 Very Dark Mahogany
- ✚ 320 Medium Pistachio Green
- V 367 Dark Pistachio Green
- − 471 Light Avocado Green
- ○ 472 Very Light Avocado Green
- — 895 Dark Christmas Green backstitch

FAIRY SLIPPER ▶

DMC #

- ✚ 320 Medium Pistachio Green
- V 367 Dark Pistachio Green
- — 895 Dark Christmas Green backstitch
- ‖ 744 Medium Yellow
- X 3687 Mauve
- M 3688 Medium Light Mauve
- • 3689 Light Mauve

Work letters and veins in leaves in backstitch with 895 Dark Christmas Green. Work tip of right-hand flower in backstitch with 3687 Mauve.

TANSY ▶

DMC #

- ⊼ 300 Very Dark Mahogany
- ⊞ 320 Medium Pistachio Green
- Ⅴ 367 Dark Pistachio Green
- ☰ 895 Dark Christmas Green
- Ⓚ 725 Topaz
- Ⅲ 744 Medium Yellow

Work letters in backstitch with 895 Dark Christmas Green.

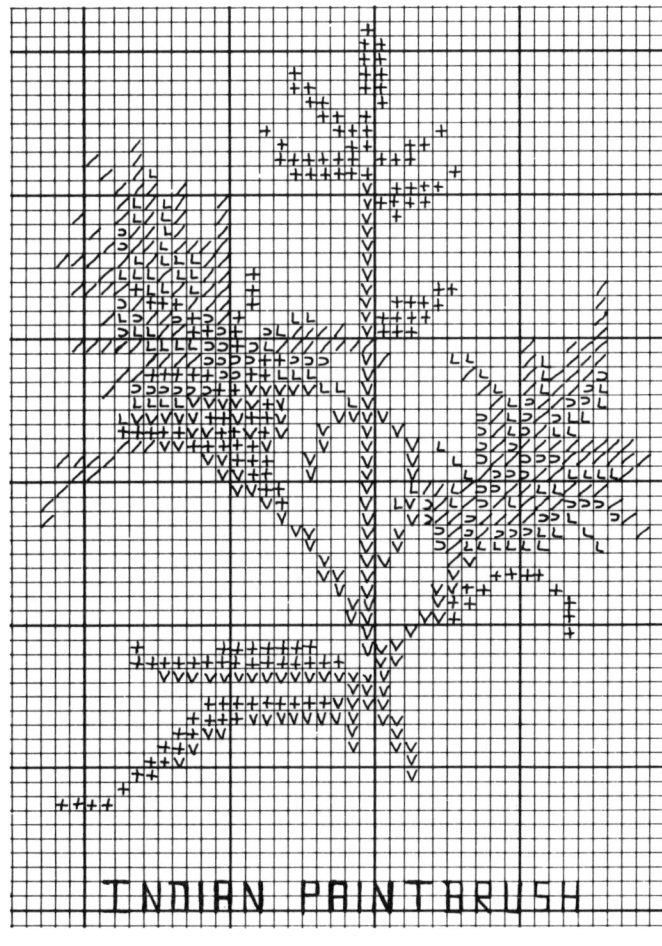

◀ INDIAN PAINTBRUSH

DMC #

- ⊞ 320 Medium Pistachio Green
- Ⅴ 367 Dark Pistachio Green
- − 895 Dark Christmas Green backstitch
- ╱ 350 Medium Coral
- ㄴ 351 Coral
- ⊃ 498 Dark Christmas Red

◀ PRAIRIE SMOKE

DMC #

- ⊞ 320 Medium Pistachio Green
- ⊟ 895 Dark Christmas Green
- ⊠ 3687 Mauve
- ⊡ 3689 Light Mauve

Work letters in backstitch with 895 Dark Christmas Green.

GOLDENEYE ▶

DMC #

- ⋀ 300 Very Dark Mahogany
- ⋁ 367 Dark Pistachio Green
- ⊟ 895 Dark Christmas Green
- ⋀ 725 Topaz
- Ⅱ 744 Medium Yellow

Work letters in backstitch with 895 Dark Christmas Green.

Flowers of the Shore

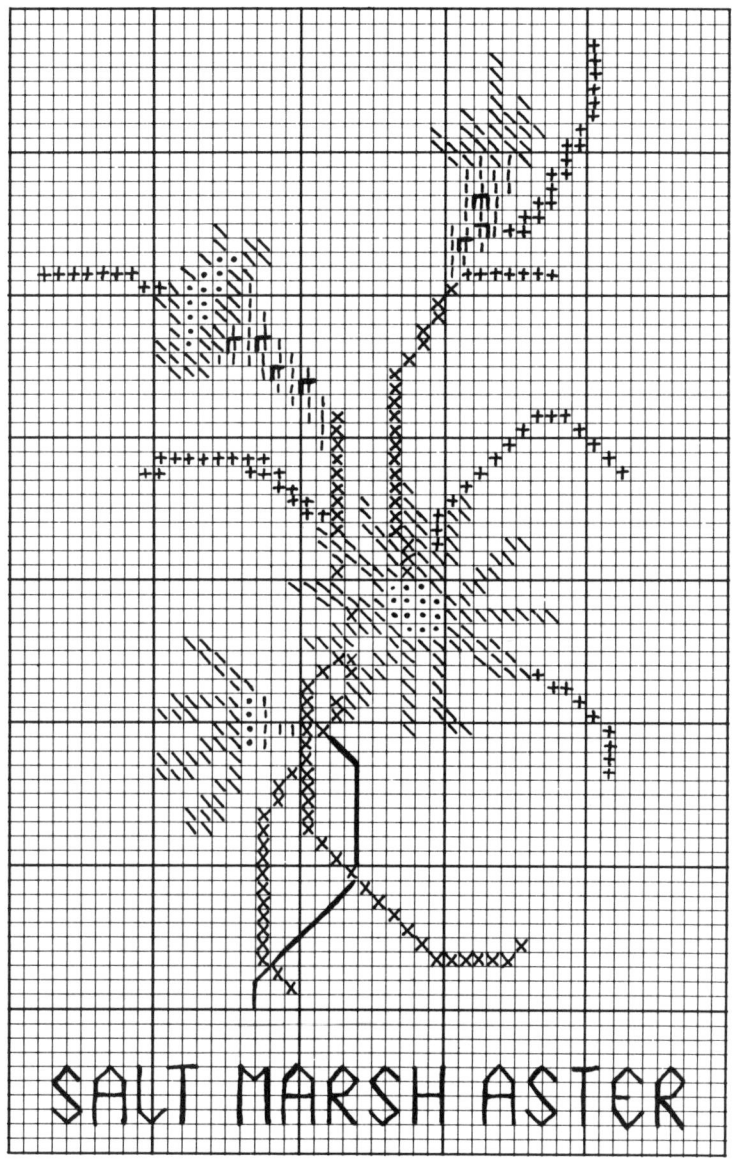

SALT MARSH ASTER

DMC #

- ◨ 210 Medium Lavender
- ⌐⌐ 434 Light Brown backstitch
- ⊡ 725 Topaz
- ☒ 3345 Dark Hunter Green
- — 3345 Dark Hunter Green backstitch
- ⊞ 3347 Medium Yellow Green
- ⊡ 3348 Light Yellow Green

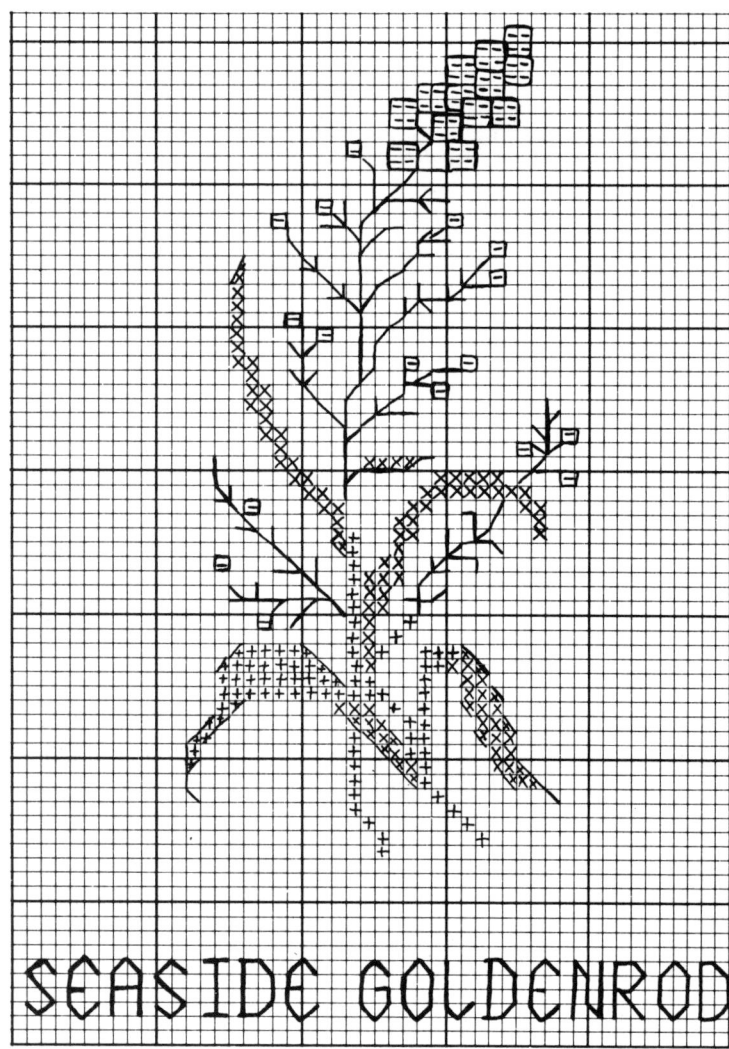

◀ SEASIDE GOLDENROD

DMC #

- — 437 Light Tan backstitch
- ⊟ 726 Light Topaz
- ☒ 3345 Dark Hunter Green
- ⊞ 3347 Medium Yellow Green

Outline Light Topaz flowers with 437 Light Tan. Work letters, stems and tips of leaves in backstitch with 3345 Dark Hunter Green. On leaves, work ¾ stitches as indicated by short diagonal lines.

SAND VERBENA ▶

DMC #

- — 434 Light Brown backstitch
- ⊡ 725 Topaz
- ⊟ 726 Light Topaz
- — 3345 Dark Hunter Green backstitch
- ⊞ 3347 Medium Yellow Green
- ⊔ 3348 Light Yellow Green

Outline flowers with 434 Light Brown; outline leaves in backstitch with 3347 Medium Yellow Green. Work letters and veins in leaves with 3345 Dark Hunter Green.

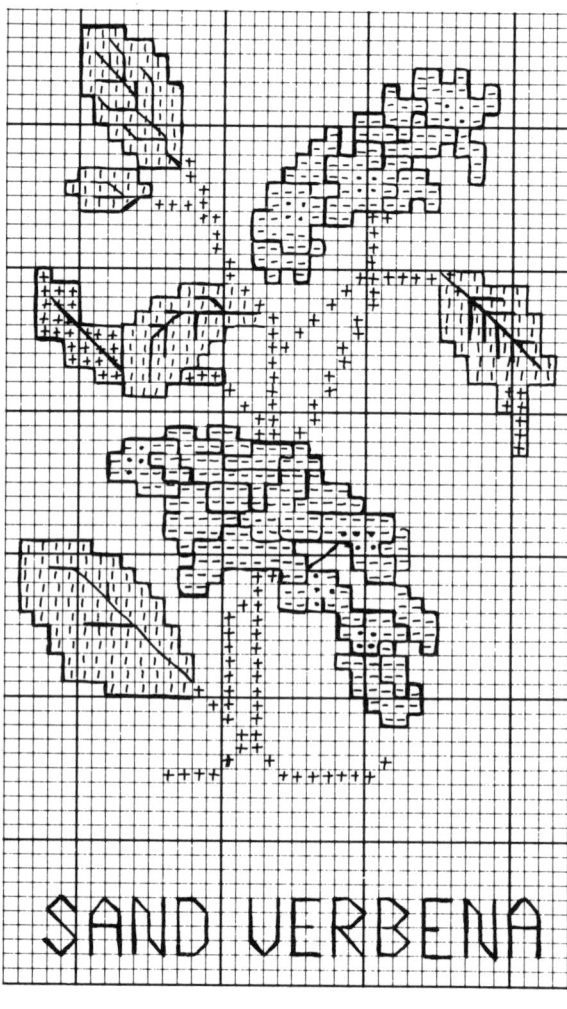

BUR REED ▶

DMC #

- — 3345 Dark Hunter Green backstitch
- ⊞ 3347 Medium Yellow Green
- ⊡ 3348 Light Yellow Green

For blossoms, combine 3345 Dark Hunter Green and 3348 Light Yellow Green in needle and take long straight stitches as indicated. Work tips of reeds in backstitch in 3347 Medium Yellow Green or 3348 Light Yellow Green. Work letters with 3345 Dark Hunter Green.

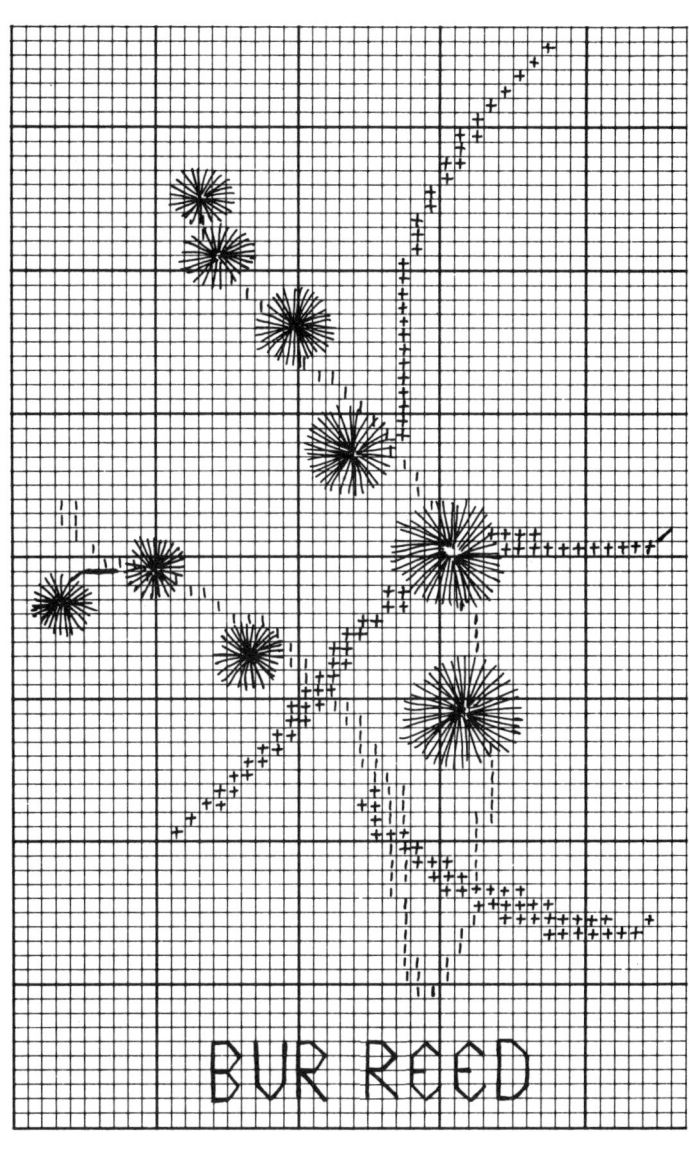

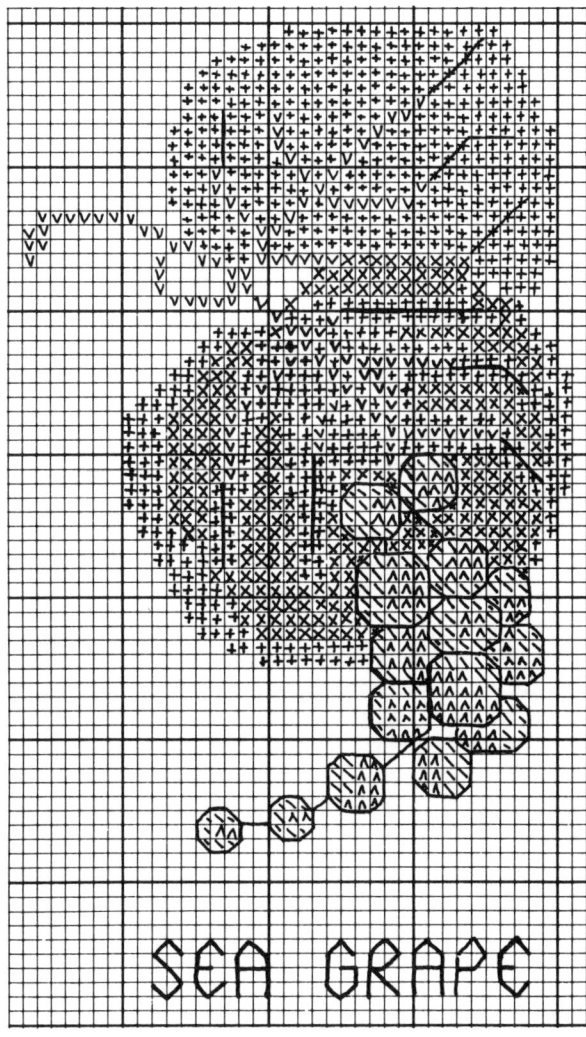

◀ SEA GRAPE

DMC #

- ⒶA 208 Very Dark Lavender
- ⒩ 210 Medium Lavender
- ⓥ 304 Medium Christmas Red
- ⓧ 3345 Dark Hunter Green
- ⊞ 3347 Medium Yellow Green

Work fine veins in leaves in backstitch with 304 Medium Christmas Red. Outline grapes in backstitch with 208 Very Dark Lavender. Work letters and stems in backstitch with 3345 Dark Hunter Green.

BEACH STRAWBERRY ▶

DMC #

- ☑ 304 Medium Christmas Red
- ⊟ 725 Topaz
- ☒ 3345 Dark Hunter Green
- ⊞ 3347 Medium Yellow Green
- ⊡ 3348 Light Yellow Green
- ☐ White

Outline flowers in backstitch with 3345 Dark Hunter Green; fill in with White cross stitches. Work straight stitch stamens with 725 Topaz; work a Topaz French knot at end of each stamen. Work letters in backstitch with 3345 Dark Hunter Green.

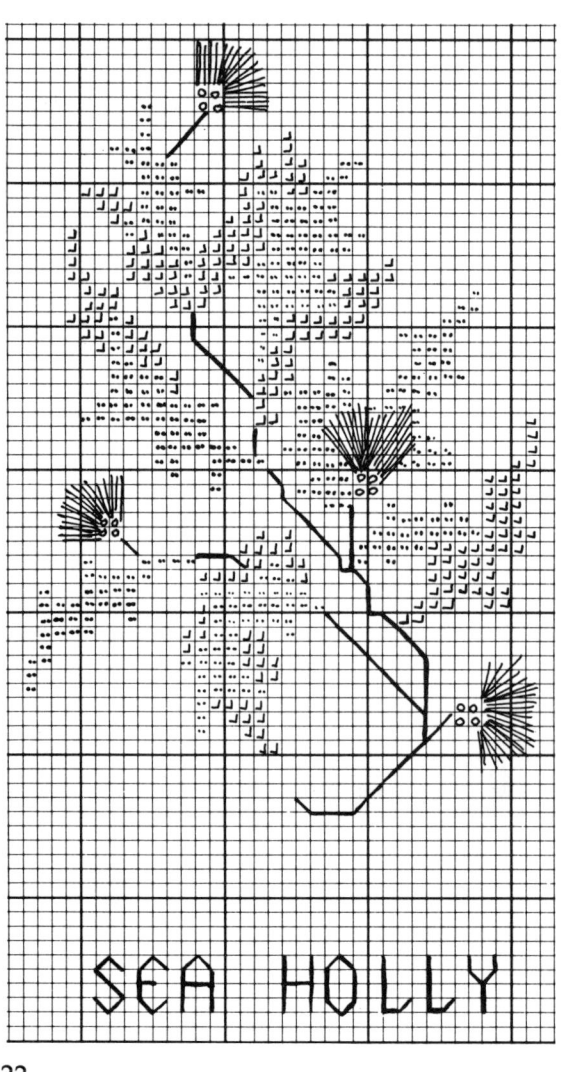

◀ SEA HOLLY

DMC #

- ⊙ { 210 Medium Lavender
- 794 Light Cornflower Blue
  Use 1 strand of each color
- ⊐ 926 Dark Gray Blue
- ⊡ 928 Light Gray Blue
- — 3345 Dark Hunter Green backstitch

For blossoms, combine 210 Medium Lavender and 794 Light Cornflower Blue in needle and work long straight stitches as indicated. Work stems in backstitch with 926 Dark Gray Blue. Work letters with 3345 Dark Hunter Green.

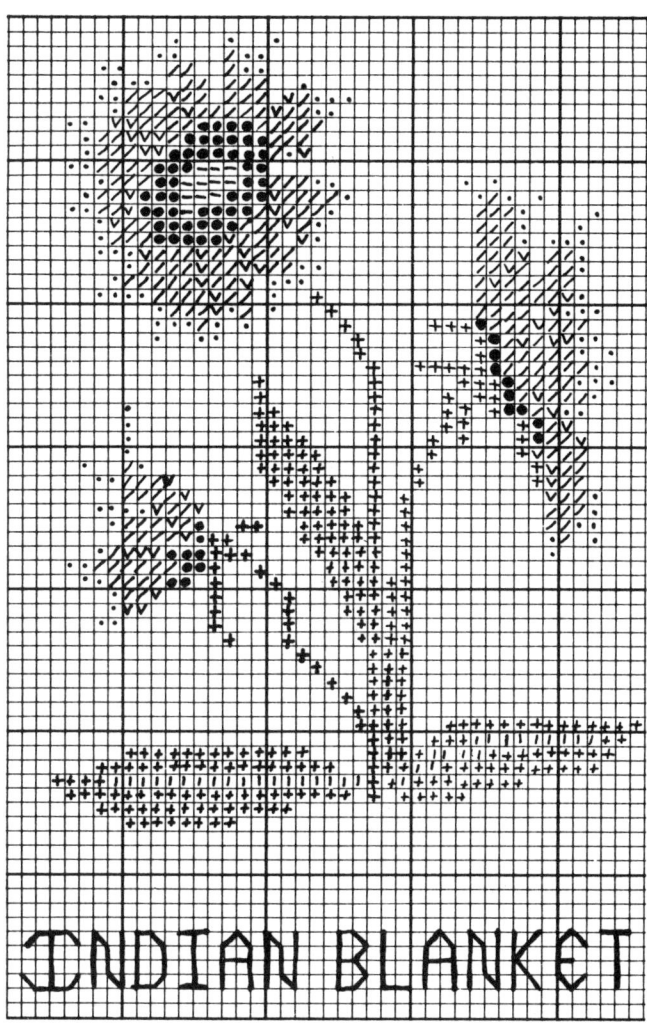

◀ **INDIAN BLANKET**

DMC #

- ⊘ 321 Christmas Red
- ☑ 304 Medium Christmas Red
- ⬤ 498 Dark Christmas Red
- · 725 Topaz
- − 726 Light Topaz
- — 3345 Dark Hunter Green backstitch
- ⊞ 3347 Medium Yellow Green
- ⊔ 3348 Light Yellow Green

SEA OATS ▶

DMC #

- Z 437 Light Tan
- — 3345 Dark Hunter Green backstitch

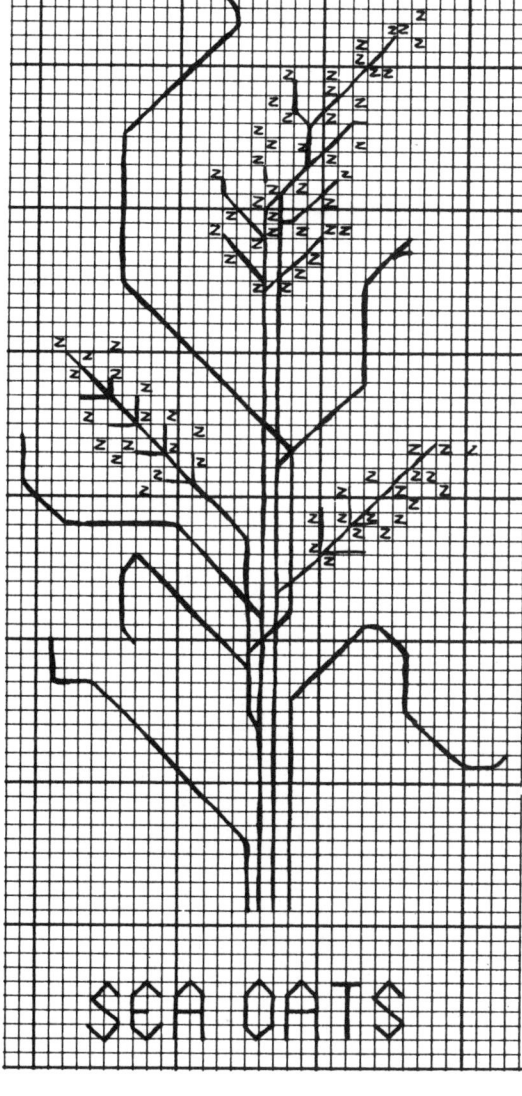

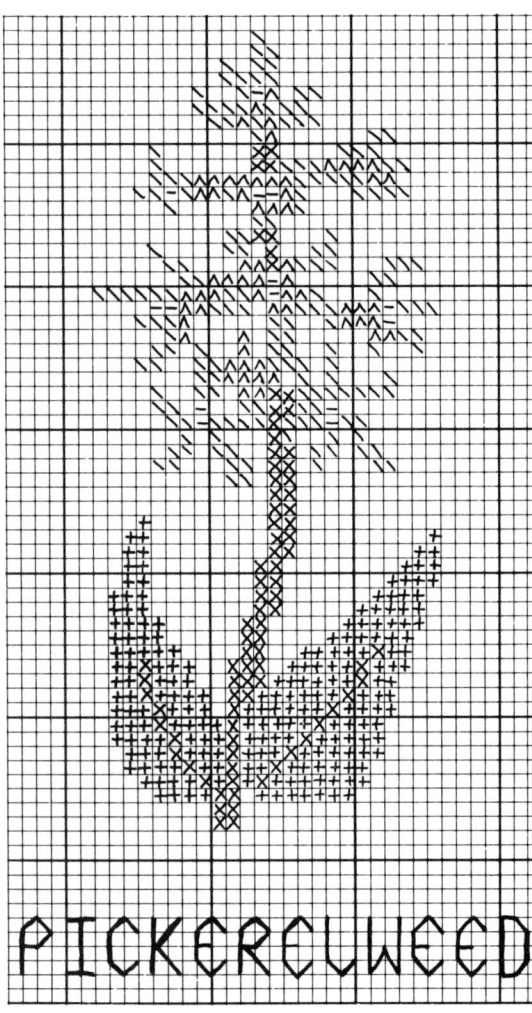

◀ **PICKERELWEED**

DMC #

- ⋀ 208 Very Dark Lavender
- ⋁ 210 Medium Lavender
- − 726 Light Topaz
- ⊠ 3345 Dark Hunter Green
- ⊞ 3347 Medium Yellow Green

Work letters in backstitch with 3345 Dark Hunter Green.

MORNING GLORY ▶

DMC #

- − 726 Light Topaz
- ═ 792 Dark Cornflower Blue
- c 793 Medium Cornflower Blue
- ‖ 794 Light Cornflower Blue
- ⊠ 3345 Dark Hunter Green
- ⊞ 3347 Medium Yellow Green

Work stems and letters in backstitch with 3345 Dark Hunter Green.

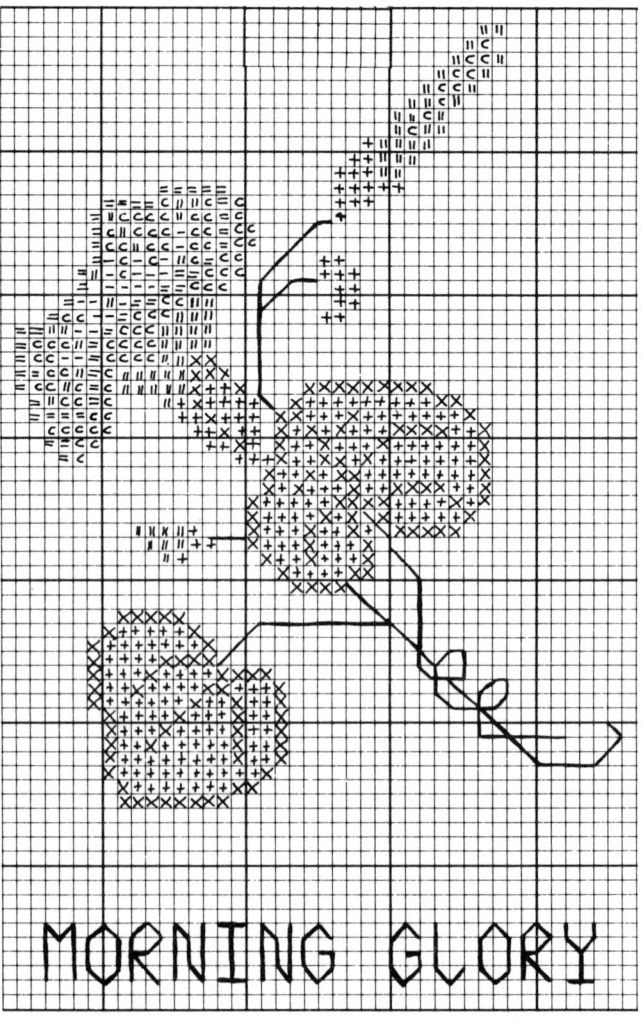

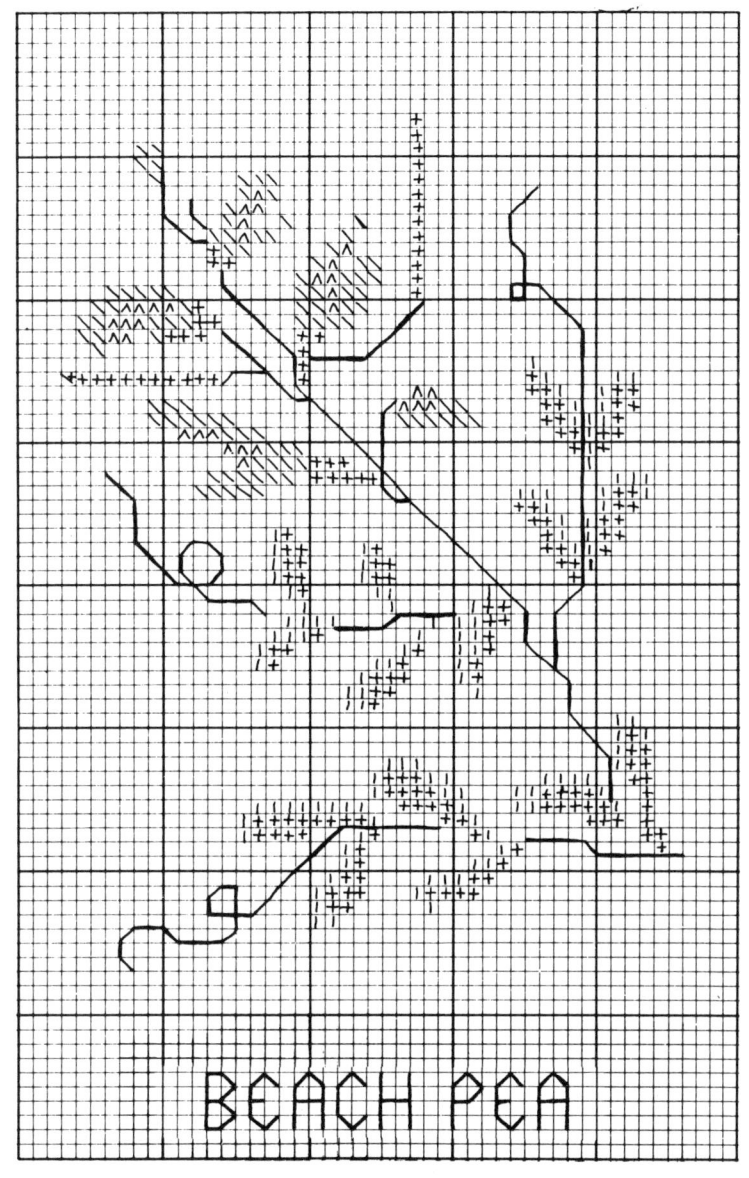

BEACH PEA

DMC #

- ⋀   208   Very Dark Lavender
- ⋁   210   Medium Lavender
- —   3345   Dark Hunter Green backstitch
- ✚   3347   Medium Yellow Green
- ❘   3348   Light Yellow Green

Flowers of the Tropics

TORCH GINGER ▶

DMC #

— 300 Very Dark Mahogany backstitch
◯ 321 Christmas Red
I 666 Bright Christmas Red
V 498 Dark Christmas Red
● 815 Medium Garnet Red
X 3345 Dark Hunter Green
+ 3347 Medium Yellow Green
∧ 3348 Light Yellow Green

◀ **GARDENIA**

DMC #

— 300 Very Dark Mahogany backstitch
— 318 Light Steel Gray backstitch
X 3345 Dark Hunter Green
+ 3347 Medium Yellow Green
· White

Outline petals with 318 Light Steel Gray; work letters with 300 Very Dark Mahogany.

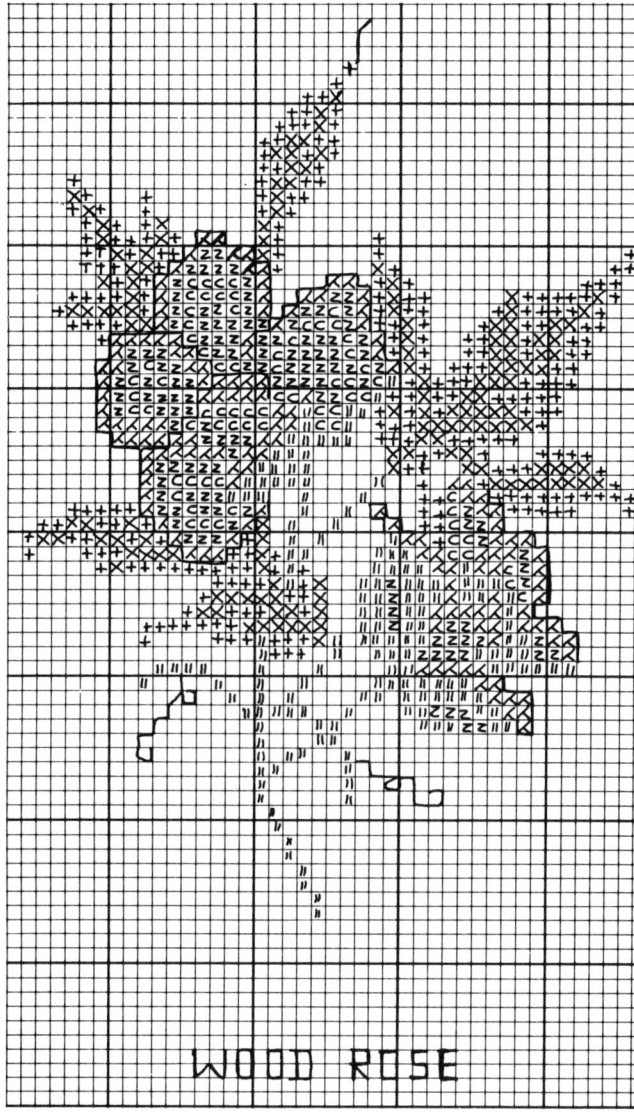

◀ WOOD ROSE

DMC #

- — 300 Very Dark Mahogany backstitch
- ⊔ 434 Light Brown
- c 437 Light Tan
- z 738 Very Light Tan
- ⋌ 739 Fawn Beige
- ⊠ 3345 Dark Hunter Green
- ⊞ 3347 Medium Yellow Green

Outline petals in backstitch with 437 Light Tan. Work tendrils on stem in backstitch with 434 Light Brown and tip of leaf in backstitch with 3345 Dark Hunter Green; work letters in backstitch with 300 Very Dark Mahogany.

BIRD OF PARADISE ▶

DMC #

- T 300 Very Dark Mahogany
- ⊔ 740 Tangerine
- W 742 Light Tangerine
- Y 743 Dark Yellow
- A { 744 Medium Yellow
       793 Medium Cornflower Blue
       Use 1 strand of each color
- ∕ 794 Light Cornflower Blue
- ∖ 921 Copper
- ⊠ 3345 Dark Hunter Green
- ⊞ 3347 Medium Yellow Green
- ⋋ 3348 Light Yellow Green

Work letters in backstitch with 300 Very Dark Mahogany.

27

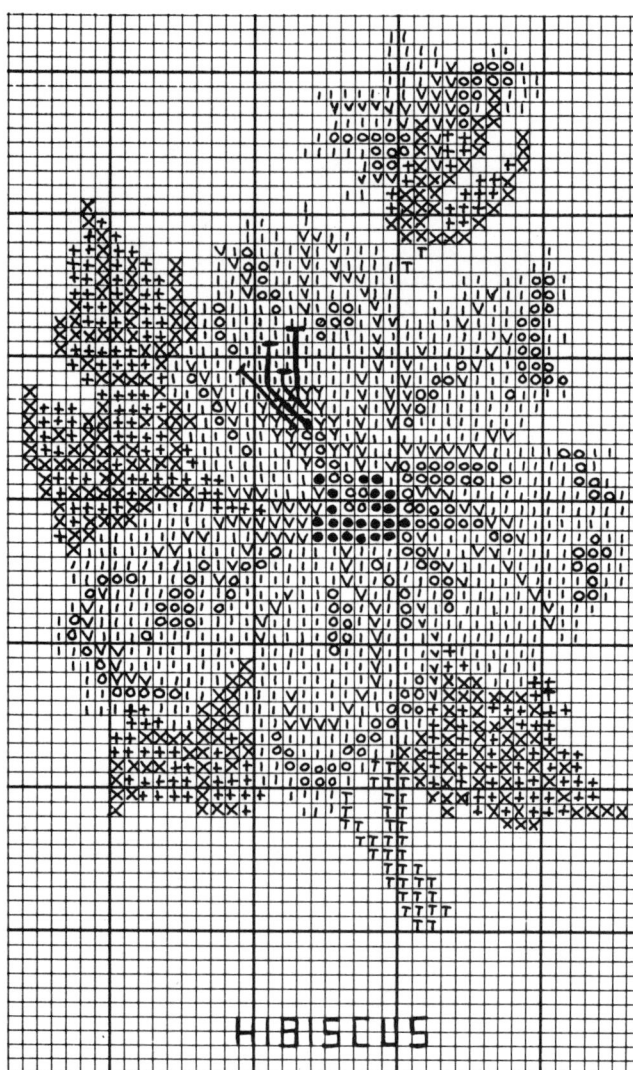

◀ HIBISCUS

DMC #

T	300	Very Dark Mahogany
O	321	Christmas Red
I	666	Bright Christmas Red
V	498	Dark Christmas Red
●	815	Medium Garnet Red
Y	743	Dark Yellow
X	3345	Dark Hunter Green
+	3347	Medium Yellow Green

Outline petals in backstitch with 815 Medium Garnet Red. Work straight stitch stamens with 743 Dark Yellow. Work letters in backstitch with 300 Very Dark Mahogany.

ANTHURIUM ▶

DMC #

—	300	Very Dark Mahogany backstitch
O	321	Christmas Red
I	666	Bright Christmas Red
V	498	Dark Christmas Red
●	815	Medium Garnet Red
Y	743	Dark Yellow
X	3345	Dark Hunter Green
+	3347	Medium Yellow Green

Outline Red leaf in backstitch with 815 Medium Garnet Red; work letters with 300 Very Dark Mahogany.

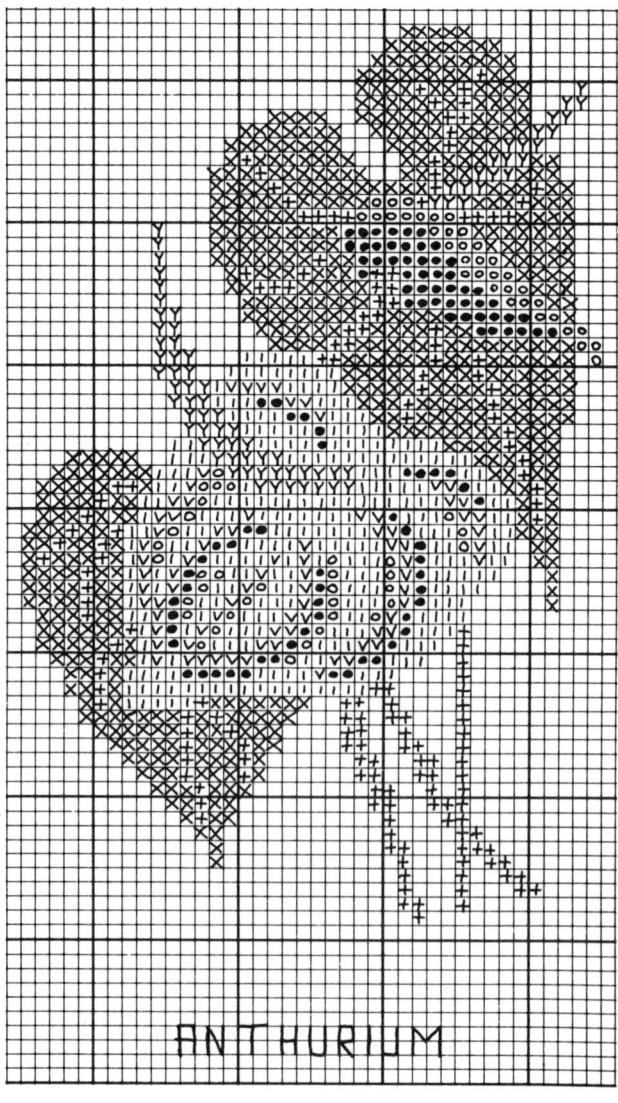

ALAMANDA ▶

DMC #

- — 300 Very Dark Mahogany backstitch
- W 742 Light Tangerine
- Y 743 Dark Yellow
- – 744 Medium Yellow
- X 3345 Dark Hunter Green
- + 3347 Medium Yellow Green
- ∧ 3348 Light Hunter Green

Outline petals in backstitch with 742 Light Tangerine; work letters with 300 Very Dark Mahogany.

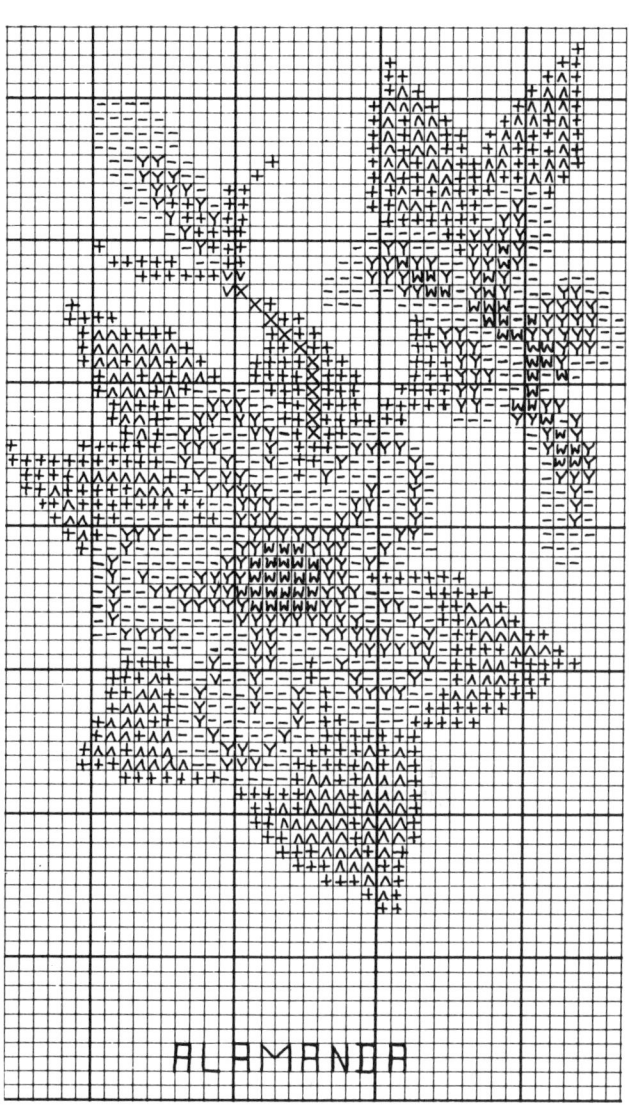

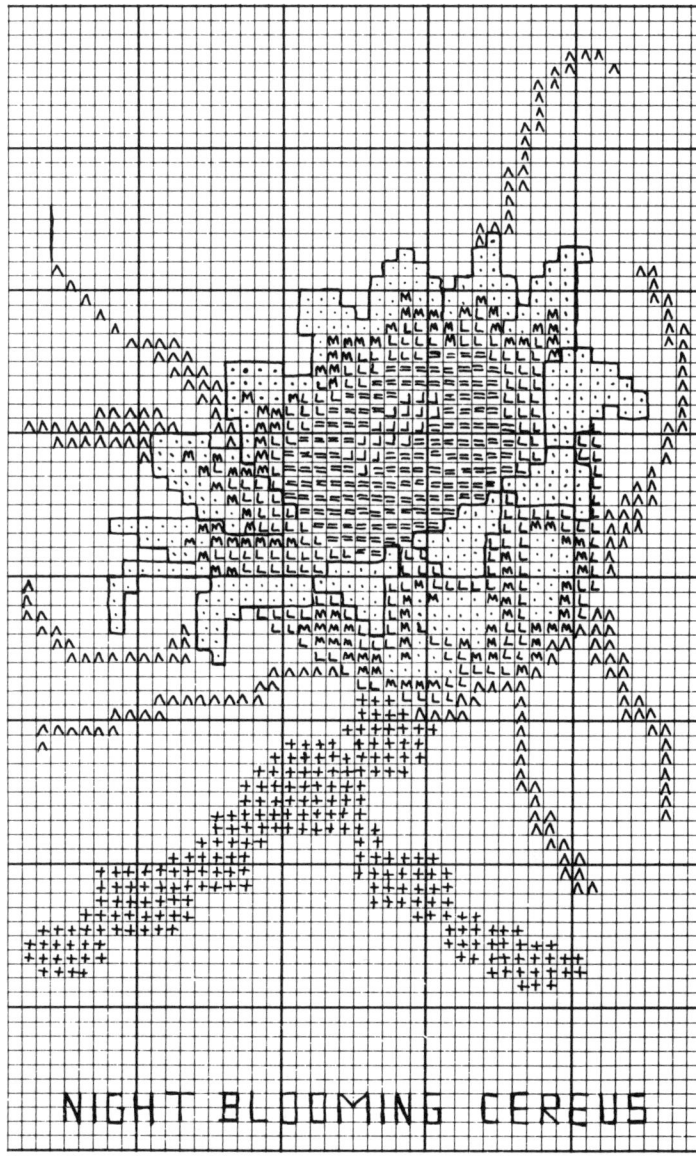

◀ NIGHT BLOOMING CEREUS

DMC #

- — 300 Very Dark Mahogany backstitch
- — 644 Medium Beige Gray backstitch
- M 712 Cream
- = 726 Light Topaz
- ⌐ 783 Christmas Gold
- + 3347 Medium Yellow Green
- ∧ 3348 Light Yellow Green
- · White
- L Ecru

Outline petals with 644 Medium Beige Gray; work letters with 300 Very Dark Mahogany.

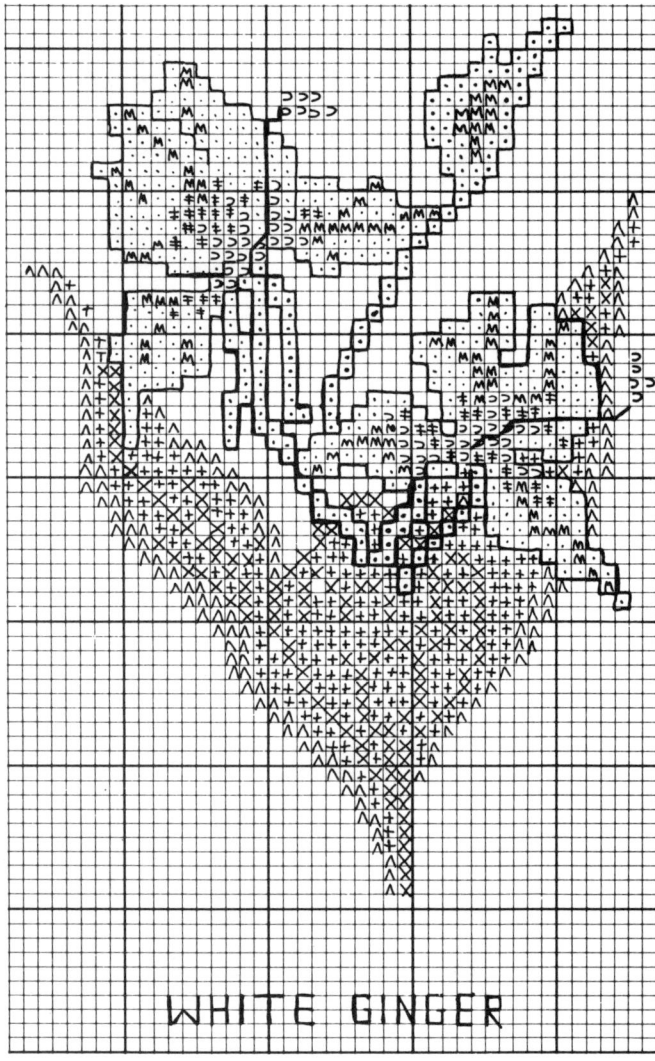

◀ WHITE GINGER

DMC #

- — 300 Very Dark Mahogany backstitch
- — 437 Light Tan backstitch
- M 712 Cream
- ⊃ 725 Topaz
- ‡ 727 Very Light Topaz
- X 3345 Dark Hunter Green
- ⊞ 3347 Medium Yellow Green
- ∧ 3348 Light Yellow Green
- · White

Outline petals with 437 Light Tan; work letters with 300 Very Dark Mahogany.

PLUMERIA ▶

DMC #

- T 300 Very Dark Mahogany
- P 776 Medium Pink
- U 818 Baby Pink
- K 899 Medium Rose
- X 3345 Dark Hunter Green
- ⊞ 3347 Medium Yellow Green
- ∧ 3348 Light Yellow Green

Outline petals in backstitch with 899 Medium Rose. Work letters in backstitch with 300 Very Dark Mahogany; work fine veins in leaves in backstitch with 3345 Dark Hunter Green.

LEHUA ▶

DMC #

T	300	Very Dark Mahogany
	321	Christmas Red
	498	Dark Christmas Red
		Use 1 strand of each color
●	815	Medium Garnet Red
⊞	3347	Medium Yellow Green
∧	3348	Light Yellow Green

For blossoms, combine 321 Christmas Red and 498 Dark Christmas Red in needle and take long straight stitches as indicated. Work stems and letters in backstitch with 300 Very Dark Mahogany.

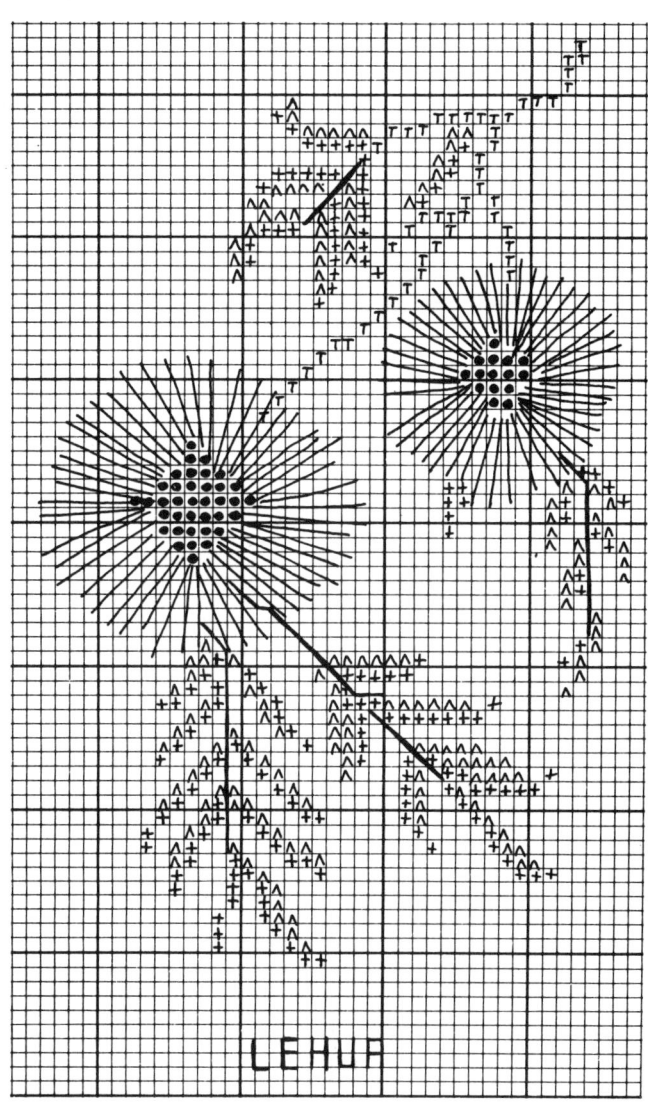

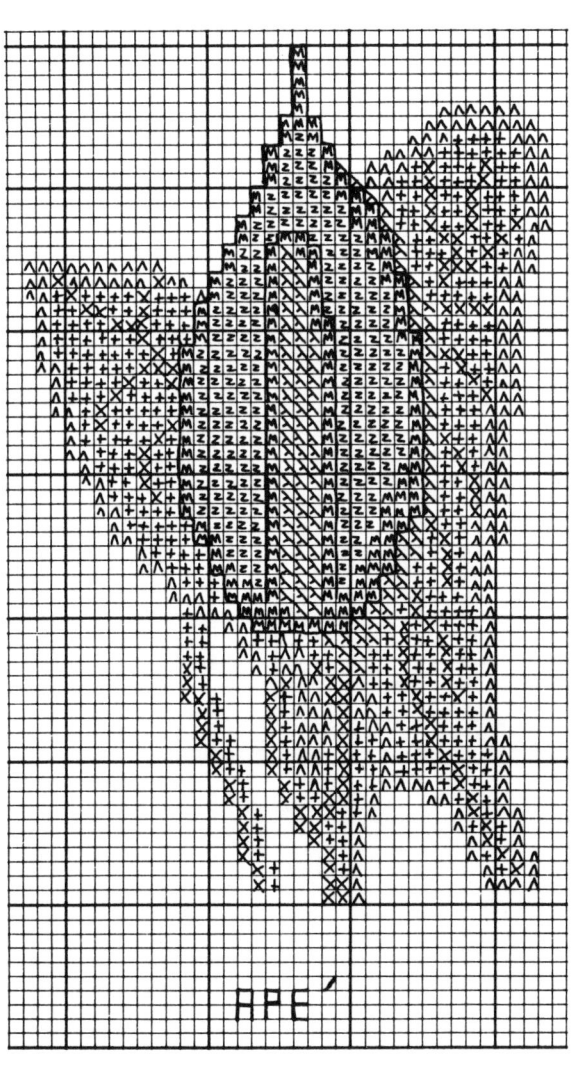

◀ APÉ

DMC #

—	300	Very Dark Mahogany backstitch
—	437	Light Tan backstitch
M	712	Cream
Z	738	Very Light Tan
⅄	948	Very Light Peach
X	3345	Dark Hunter Green
⊞	3347	Medium Yellow Green
∧	3348	Light Yellow Green

Outline flower with 437 Light Tan; work letters with 300 Very Dark Mahogany.

31

SIX STRAND EMBROIDERY COTTON (FLOSS) CONVERSION CHART

KEY: T = Possible Substitute   * = Close Match   — = No Match

DMC NO.	ROYAL MOULINÉ NO.	BATES/ANCHOR NO.
White	1001	2
Ecru	8600	926
208	3335*	110*
209	3415*	105
210	3320*	104
211	3410	108*
221	2570	897*
223	2555	894
224	2545	893
225	2540	892
300	8330	352*
301	8315*	349*
304	2415*	47*
307	6005*	289*
309	2525*	42*
310	1002	403
311	4275T	149*
312	—	147*
315	3130	896*
316	3120	895*
317	1030*	400*
318	1020*	399*
319	5025	246*
320	5015	216*
321	2415	47
322	—	978*
326	2530*	59*
327	3365*	101*
333	—	119
334	4250T	145
335	2525T	42*
336	4270*	149*
340	—	118
341	—	117
347	2425*	13*
349	2400	13
350	2045T	11
351	2015T	11*
352	2015	10*
353	2010*	8*
355	8095	5968
356	8090	5975*
367	5020	216*
368	5005*	240*
369	5005	213*
370	—	889*
371	—	888*
372	—	887*
400	8325*	351
402	8305*	347*
407	8005	882*
413	1025*	401
414	1020*	400*
415	1015	398
420	8720*	375*
422	8710*	373*
433	8265	371*
434	8215	309
435	8210*	369*
436	8205	363*

DMC NO.	ROYAL MOULINÉ NO.	BATES/ANCHOR NO.
437	8200*	362
444	6155*	291
445	6000	288
451	—	399*
452	—	399*
453	1015T	397*
469	5255	267*
470	5255*	267
471	5245	266*
472	5240	264*
498	2425T	20*
500	5125	879*
501	5120*	878
502	5110	876
503	5105	875
504	5100	213*
517	—	169*
518	4860*	168*
519	4855T	167*
520	—	862*
522	—	859*
523	—	859*
524	—	858*
535	1115T	401*
543	8500	933*
550	3380*	102*
552	3370*	101
553	3360	98
554	3355*	96*
561	—	212*
562	—	210*
563	—	208*
564	—	203*
580	5935	267*
581	5925	266*
597	4860*	168*
598	4855*	167*
600	2225*	59*
601	2225*	78*
602	2640*	77*
603	2720*	76*
604	2710	75*
605	2155	50*
606	7260	335
608	7255	333*
610	5825T	889*
611	5735T	898
612	8815*	832
613	5605*	956*
632	8530	936*
640	8625	903
642	8620*	392
644	8800	830
645	1115	905*
646	1115*	8581
647	1110	8581*
648	1100*	900
666	2405	46
676	6250	891
677	—	886*

DMC NO.	ROYAL MOULINÉ NO.	BATES/ANCHOR NO.
680	6260*	901
699	5375	923*
700	5365*	229
701	5365*	227
702	5330	239
703	5320	238
704	5310*	256*
712	8600*	387*
718	3015*	88
720	—	326
721	—	324*
722	—	323*
725	6215	306*
726	6150*	295
727	6135	293
729	6255	890
730	—	924*
731	—	281*
732	5925T	281*
733	—	280*
734	—	279*
738	8245*	942
739	8240*	885*
740	7045	316
741	6125	304
742	6120	303
743	6210	297
744	6110*	301*
745	6105	300*
746	6100	386*
747	4850	158*
754	8075	778*
758	8080	868
760	2035	9*
761	2030	8*
762	1010*	397
772	—	264*
775	4600*	128*
776	2110*	24*
778	3110	968*
780	8215*	310*
781	8215	309*
782	6230	308
783	6220*	307
791	4165*	941
792	4155T	940
793	4155	121
794	4145	120*
796	4340	133*
797	4265*	132*
798	4325	131*
799	4250*	130*
800	4310	128
801	8405	357*
806	4810T	169*
807	4860*	168*
809	4145*	130*
813	4610*	160*
814	2340T	44*
815	2530*	43

DMC NO.	ROYAL MOULINÉ NO.	BATES/ANCHOR NO.
816	2530	44*
817	2415T	19
818	2505*	48
819	2000	892*
820	4345	134
822	8605*	387*
823	4400*	150
824	4225	164*
825	4215	162*
826	4210	161*
827	4605	159*
828	4850	158*
829	5825	906
830	5825T	889*
831	5825T	889*
832	5815	907
833	5815*	874*
834	5810*	874
838	8425T	380*
839	8560	380*
840	8555	379*
841	8550	378*
842	8505	376*
844	1115T	401*
869	8720*	944*
890	5025*	879*
891	2135	35*
892	2130	28
893	2125*	27
894	2115T	26
895	5430*	246*
898	8425*	360
899	2515	27*
900	7230*	333
902	—	72*
904	5295*	258*
905	5295	258*
906	5285*	256*
907	5280*	255
909	5370	229*
910	5370*	228*
911	5465*	205*
912	5465	205
913	5460*	209
915	3030	89*
917	3020*	89*
918	8330*	341*
919	8095*	341*
920	8060*	339*
921	8060T	349*
922	8315T	324*
924	4830T	851*
926	4820*	779*
927	4810T	849*
928	1010T	900*
930	4510	922*
931	4505	921*
932	4500	920*
934	5070T	862*
935	5225T	159*

DMC NO.	ROYAL MOULINÉ NO.	BATES/ANCHOR NO.
936	5260*	269
937	5260	268
938	8430	381
939	4405	127
943	4935*	188*
945	8020*	347*
946	7230*	332*
947	7255*	330*
948	8070	778*
950	8020T	4146
951	8020T	366*
954	5455*	203*
955	5450	206*
956	2170*	40*
957	2160T	40*
958	—	187
959	2515*	186
961	2515	76*
962	2505	76*
963	—	49*
964	5150*	185
966	7040	214*
970	7045	316*
971	—	316*
972	6120*	298
973	6015	290
975	8365	355*
976	8355	308*
977	8350	307*
986	5430	246*
987	5020T	244*
988	5295T	243*
989	5405T	242*
991	5165T	189*
992	4925*	187*
993	4915*	186*
995	4710	410
996	4700	433
3011	5525T	845*
3012	5525*	844*
3013	5515	842*
3021	5430	382*
3022	5020T	8581*
3023	5295T	8581*
3024	5460*	900*
3031	1100	905*
3032	8620T	903*
3033	8610*	388*
3041	3215*	871
3042	3205*	869
3045	6260T	373*
3046	5810	887*
3047	5805	886*
3051	5530T	846*
3052	5060*	859*
3053	5055*	859*
3064	8005*	914*
3072	4805*	397*
3078	6130	292*
3325	4200	159*

DMC NO.	ROYAL MOULINÉ NO.	BATES/ANCHOR NO.
3326	2115T	25*
3328	2045	11*
3340	—	329
3341	—	328
3345	5025T	268*
3346	5220T	257*
3347	5210*	266*
3348	5270*	265
3350	2220	42*
3354	2210	74*
3362	—	862*
3363	—	861*
3364	—	843*
3371	8435	382
3607	—	87*
3608	—	86
3609	—	85
3685	2335	70*
3687	2325	69*
3688	2320	66*
3689	2310	49
3705	—	35*
3706	—	28*
3708	—	26*
48	9000*	1201*
51	9014	1220
52	9006	1208
53	—	—
57	9002	1203
61	9013T	1218*
62	9000T	1201*
67	—	1211*
69	—	1218*
75	9002	1206*
90	9012T	1217*
91	9008*	1211
92	9011T	1216*
93	9007*	1210*
94	9011*	1216
95	9006T	1208*
99	9005T	1207*
101	9009*	1213*
102	—	1208*
103	—	1210*
104	9012	1217
105	9013*	1218
106	9002T	1203*
107	9003	1204
108	9014*	1220*
111	—	1218*
112	9003T	1204*
113	9007*	1210*
114	9010	1215
115	9004	1206
121	9007	1210
122	9010T	1215*
123	—	1213*
124	9007T	1210*
125	9009	1213
126	9006*	1208*

Reproduced by permission of the copyright owner, The American School of Needlework, Inc.